THE END OF BELONGING
Untold stories of leaving home and the psychology of global relocation

Revised January, 2010

All rights reserved.
Copyright © 2009, by Greg A Madison, Ph D.
No part of this book may be reproduced or transmitted in any form or by any means, electronic or mechanical, including photocopying, recording, or by any information storage and retrieval system, without permission in writing from the publisher.

THE END OF BELONGING

Untold stories of leaving home and the psychology of global relocation

Why spurn my home when exile is your home?
The Ithaca you want you'll have in not having.
You'll walk her shores yet long to tread those very grounds,
kiss Penelope yet wish you held your wife instead,
touch her flesh yet yearn for mine.
Your home's in the rubblehouse of time now,
and you're made thus, to yearn for what you lose.

Andre Aciman, *Out of Egypt: A Memoir* (1994)

Greg A Madison, PhD
London England

Dedication:

This book is dedicated to those of us who alternate between the wayward and the defiant, whose deeper motivations for leaving home have been misunderstood or silenced. The writing of this book would be worthwhile if even a single reader finds herein some acknowledgment of the significance of their need to leave, and thereby, even fleetingly, felt the possibility of belonging.

The book is also dedicated with appreciation and love to my father and my mother, who didn't have to understand my decisions in order to support me, and who withstood many painful moments at airport departures without ever trying to stop me.

Thank you.

THE END OF BELONGING

Introduction: View from a Calcutta Roof 7

PART ONE – DISCOVERING A WAY OF BEING

1. The missing stories of leaving home 13
2. The gap in understanding 18
3. The depth of the question 22
4. Preparing to listen 27
5. The Budapest months 34
6. Themes of existential migration 41
   6.1 Who am I? 42
   6.2 Where do I belong? 47
   6.3 What do I value in life? 61
   6.4 A worldwide perspective 68
   6.5 Love of difference and foreignness 72
   6.6 Origins - early family and home circumstances 82
   6.7 Main issues of home and homecoming 92
   6.8 The drama and paradox of leaving 105
7. The poignant predicament 121
8. A tale of existential migration 125

PART TWO - A NEW PSYCHOLOGY OF LEAVING HOME AND THE ADVENT OF GLOBAL HOMELESSNESS

9. Self-identity, belonging and home 131
   9.1 What is a person? 132
   9.2 Belonging 137
   9.3 Conceptions of home 142
10. A philosophy of dwelling and homecoming 156
    10.1 Homeworld and alienworld 159
    10.2 World alienation and the unheimlich 164
    10.3 Dwelling and homecoming 172
11. Sensitivities in existential migration 184
    11.1 Practical implications 187
12. Leaving and individual psychology 194
13. Existential migration and autobiographies of exile 199
14. Final cautionary thoughts 208

BIBLIOGRAPHY 214
INDEX 220

INTRODUCTION
VIEW FROM A CALCUTTA ROOF

This book is based upon individual stories of leaving home; autobiographies of homelessness by unsettled people who move from place to place, country to country, in search of fulfilment. I am one of those people, both fortunate and unfortunate, as perhaps are you. There are many like us, increasingly many all around the world, who share this deep invisible affinity. We are a community that lurks on the edge of community, without a sense of belonging, a community that shuns its own existence. We are an alternative human history, unrecorded and unacknowledged even by ourselves, until now. These are our haunting accounts of life, adventure, longing, and loss. Within these stories is an implicit warning to a world that seems on the verge of destroying its capacity to be a home for us, to offer us any sense of belonging.

The *existential migrant*, the term I use to describe us, chooses to leave his or her homeland, pushed out by deep questions that can't be answered at home, pulled into the wide world in order to discover what life is. We are living paradoxes. We need to feel at home but have never done so, we need to belong but renounce opportunities for belonging, we venture out into the unknown in order to experience the homecoming that will finally settle us, but doesn't.

The substance of this book was uncovered quite by accident during intensive interviews with twenty people who had chosen to leave home to live in a foreign country. The content of those interviews has subsequently been confirmed by numerous other voluntary migrants, some of whom are also psychology or migration researchers. Those initial twenty interviews were part of an original research project that took place in London at the turn of the 20th century and culminated in the new term 'existential migration' which will be described later. This book is not the result of abstract theories or post-modern speculation. This book is based upon the actual accounts of leaving, arriving, staying, returning, and the better understanding that those people gave me of my own restlessness, wandering, and longing. Whether you have left home, are desperate to leave home, never found home, have been unexpectedly unsettled by moving to another culture, or have accidentally found yourself lost in the world, I hope that reading these experiences will offer some succour or at least encourage you to speak about your own experiences of leaving and not belonging.

Before I started research into the experience of voluntary migrants I had already spent a year researching the experience of young doctors working in an inner city London hospital. The radical turn in attention, from studying medical staff to exploring voluntary migration, crystallized during a two-week visit to Calcutta and Kathmandu; two weeks which instigated a profound and transformative shift in me. It is worth mentioning some specifics of that trip since it somehow drew to the surface a nascent experience of 'homelessness' that had been formulating un-thought within me over years. In retrospect, I realize that the profound issue of not-being-at-home has always been a powerful undercurrent in my life, guiding much more than the research project and this book.

In spring 2001 I took a break from the stressful confines of my hospital work and travelled to Asia at the invitation of a friend who was temporarily living in Calcutta. I was excited to travel to a place that I

INTRODUCTION : VIEW FROM A CALCUTTA ROOF

anticipated would be deeply foreign and unfamiliar compared to the life I was then leading in London. My first glimpse of India shocked and inspired me. Waking early on the first morning after my arrival, I wandered onto the roof terrace to gaze upon the city that I had seen only through the darkness of my arrival the night before. That arrival itself was eventful, my friend and I were threatened at gunpoint by a troop of drunken police officers who had flagged down our taxi on the road from the airport into town. After extricating ourselves from that rather bizarre and quite frightening episode, my friend and I continued along the dark road into Calcutta, past countless open fires dotted along the ditches all the way into the nebulous city centre. The scene created, for me at least, a very atmospheric, opaque dream-like feeling, enhanced by the disorientation of jetlag and the adrenaline of having just had a revolver in my face. The next morning on the roof garden, I was half confirming that the evening before had in fact occurred; that I really was waking up in this alien world of Calcutta.

As I searched the morning skyline, I was unable to draw upon much in my previous experience that could reference what I observed. There was *something* in this colourful and chaotic foreignness that enthralled me. I had dreamed that perhaps someplace so utterly alien still existed on earth; it was an unexpected *relief* to be surveying a city so totally *other*, not even a Coke sign to betray that it belonged on the same planet as the western world I had left behind; but why *relief*? At first my responses, being mine, seemed quite unremarkable but after some reflection with my friend, who had similar responses to travel, we both began to wonder why we felt what we felt and began to realize that not everyone would feel what we felt sat on that Calcutta rooftop.

Thus commenced a two-week contemplative-adventure, deep and authentic travel, characterized by an incessant dialogue with my friend regarding the allure of the foreign, the compulsion to explore the diversity of the world, and the strange experience of travelling through liminal spaces like airports and border crossings. These attractions were superimposed upon a distinct undercurrent of repulsion regarding conventional settled life. I returned to London with the conviction that the question of home; the motivations for leaving home to live in foreign places, and the underlying question of being at-home in the world at all, constituted the appropriate topic for my research. I realize now that these questions have imbued most if not all of my major life choices; a phenomenon that with even a little contemplation became totally perplexing. I did not approach the topic with a hypothesis regarding *why* people chose to leave their homes to live in strange lands, rather I genuinely wanted to discover whether there was anything to investigate at all in this act of leaving. It was possible to me that I, or perhaps my friend and I, were the only ones who floundered upon inscrutability at every attempt to understand our restlessness and our fascination with the unfamiliar.

I was somewhat apprehensive that we were overlooking something obvious, yet every obvious explanation, including the elaborate psychological theories, seemed to unravel when compared with our own lived experiences. In discussions with my friend the mystery had deepened, not dissipated, and during our second week in Kathmandu I was already tentatively observing fellow travellers trying to identify which ones were engaged in what I later came to call 'existential migration' and which were short-term tourists in the more conventional sense. I felt that somehow I could make speculative judgments about membership of this unacknowledged 'tribe' – he or she tended to sit slightly apart from the crowd, favouring the 'authentic experience' over the beaten track, gazing into an 'inner distance' while eager to be unobtrusive and nearly invisible, preoccupied by the internal responses to the foreignness all around them. Some of these initial intuitions seemed consistent with what later emerged from the research interviews.

Part One
Discovering a way of being

CHAPTER 1
THE MISSING STORIES OF LEAVING HOME

In the literature on moving from country to country, the actual experience of the individuals involved in these migrations is largely absent. With the exception of a few evocative autobiographies, notable among them Eva Hoffman's *Lost in Translation* and Edward Said's memoir *Out of Place*, the lived experience of migration has been neglected, especially so in the mainstream psychological, psychotherapeutic, and social science literature. The literature that does exist, including the autobiographies cited above, mostly focus on individuals who have been forced into exile by political and social circumstances, or pressed to migrate (as a child in Hoffman's case) in search of a better standard of living or advanced education (as in Said's case), rather than those who, *for some reason choose* to make themselves 'foreigners'. It is not uncommon for voluntary migrants to cope with a decreased standard of living as a result of leaving their homeland, demonstrating that their motive for departure is not primarily economic.

At the beginning of the 21st century, the individuals who *choose* to leave their homeland constitute a growing subgroup of those who leave home to live, even temporarily, in a foreign place. These individuals are not refugees in the accepted sense: they could have stayed and they can return, at least from a spectator viewpoint. It is interesting that in the following stories most participants adamantly insist that they *couldn't* have stayed, they *had to* go (though as a result of internal rather than external compulsion) and despite significant hardship in some cases, not one person regretted their choice to leave. Yet it is unclear what motivates an individual to abandon their familiar place of origin, and in some cases comfortable standard of living, in favour of becoming in the words of the psychologist Harriett Goldenberg, 'a stranger in a strange land'.

In the few cursory glances at *voluntary* migrants, it has been assumed that their individual motivation is explained by their personal psychology; their leaving is symptomatic of how they have reacted to difficult relationships within the home environment. The 'mental health' difficulties that can arise as a consequence of migration are therefore thought of as 'problems' within the individual. There may be a modicum of truth to these speculations, more so in some cases than others. However, as an explanation for leaving, family dysfunction offers a woefully inadequate response to the depth of experience revealed in the excerpts of life recounted in this book.

The research study upon which this book is based was designed to systematically gather the experiences of voluntary migrants. It explores what provoked the initial leaving, what motivates those who return 'home' (or who long to return), and what happens to the person and their whole concept of 'home' during this process. I want to move beyond the surface appearance of the processes involved to concentrate on the deeper underlying psychology of these processes. In short, I want to explore whether these stories of leaving disclose something universal about human being. If so, this study should be potentially useful for understanding migration in general, including the experiences of refugees, economic migrants, issues of international business recruitment and retention, or maybe all of us if we notice that the world is hurdling towards a global enterprize that may turn out to be the end of belonging itself.

The 21st century, with its emphasis on trans-national interventions and corporate globalization, is generating increasing demands and opportunities for a mobile workforce and therefore encouraging an unprecedented increase in the numbers of voluntary migrants. There is some evidence to suggest that these chosen cross-cultural experiences, while exciting and enriching, are not without struggle, pain, and distress[1]. Because they are chosen rather than forced, the difficulty involved in such experiences is often not anticipated by the individual and rarely acknowledged in the public domain. As the number of people coping privately and individually with these issues increases, there is a growing imperative to understand the underlying meaning of this process and the effect it can have on those who *choose* to experience it. There is a corresponding need to understand the subsequent experiences of those who eventually attempt to return 'home': is it possible to settle back into an environment that is deeply familiar but subsequently, due to inevitable change over time in both the person and the place, also peculiarly unfamiliar? The existential dynamics of voluntary migration may unveil a more ubiquitous malaise underlying our 'post-modern' world. It may be that our contemporary capitalist structure is increasingly offering confrontations with the 'homeless' underbelly of the world, voluntary migration being one potent expression of this. If so, this is an unintended side effect of globalization and one that may produce unwanted repercussions. This constitutes a powerful rationale to attempt a deeper understanding and clear exposition of the experiences and choices that are now being made for the most part unreflectively.

We will see that focusing on these people who willingly seek out

---

1. Acculturation can be difficult, involving bereavement, confusion and distress, and this is seen clearly in the refugee and asylum seeker's experience but also in the experience of voluntary migrants. Though there are significant differences between the groups, it will emerge that the act of choosing to leave does not seem to reduce the turmoil of doing so.

the unfamiliar margins may also improve our understanding of common human themes such as belonging, home and security, diversity and convention, as well as acknowledging the positive aspects of not-belonging, not feeling at home, and human insecurity. As a psychologist and psychotherapist I began to expect that deeply exploring the phenomena of being a foreigner in relation to the concept of 'home' would have implications for general theories of psychotherapy and counselling. I envisaged that many common difficulties in living, evident in the consulting room, may harbour an implicit element of the struggle for 'home', a struggle that is perhaps inherently deeply human and thus perhaps not within the realm of what can be satisfactorily 'resolved'. As the interviews suggest, the acknowledgement that happens through dialogue itself, while not providing an answer, can be positively engaging, facilitating self-understanding and new choices. It is noteworthy that the research participants overwhelmingly found that the opportunity to reflect in-depth regarding their leaving home was a valuable and positive experience, and a peculiarly emotive one. They also felt in some way transformed during this exploration.

Since the interviews were very much like a psychotherapy session, I became intrigued by the potential applicability of this form of dialogue to working with immigrants and refugees, ex-patriot communities, anthropologists engaged in foreign fieldwork, as well as NGO, corporate, diplomatic, and media staff preparing for work in international locations. Also, supportive therapeutic groups for 'trailing families' of corporate staff relocating to foreign cultures, or perhaps any group of individuals having cross-cultural contact. Cross-cultural contact is often credited with the ability to shake life assumptions and to deconstruct our everyday taken for granted attitudes about life. Much of what we assume to be natural can be revealed as purely cultural, even arbitrary. Despite the experience of 'culture shock' and its unsettling impact, when faced with foreignness the voluntary migrants I spoke with seem to experience something closer to my own experiences on the Calcutta rooftop – not shock, but relief, exhilaration, an alive and conscious awakening.

CHAPTER 2
THE GAP IN UNDERSTANDING

Eva Hoffman's *Lost in Translation* traces the darker story behind the fairy tale of immigration as triumphant progress, highlighting the loss of the '…romantic illusion of unity and centre and of the costs and rewards, the joys and the terrors, of being thrown into the postmodern world of constantly shifting boundaries and borderless possibilities'[2]. In a recent interview, Hoffman speaks of her own experience of the topsy-turvy re-arrangement of all cultural values, including 'notions of human intimacy or beauty or the distances at which we stand from each other…' She goes on to say,

> Yes, I think every immigrant becomes a kind of amateur anthropologist – you do notice things about the culture or the world that you come into that people who grow up in it, who are very embedded in it, simply don't notice. I think we all know it from going to a foreign place. And at first you notice the surface things, the surface differences. And gradually you start noticing the deeper differences. And very gradually you start with understanding the inner life of the culture, the life of those both large and very intimate values. It was a surprisingly long process is what I can say[3].

In her brief review of Peter Read's *Returning to Nothing; the meaning*

---

2. Fjellestad, 1995:135
3. Kreisler, 2000: 3

of lost places, the Australian poet Carole Rivett cites TS Eliot's remark, '*Home is where one starts from*', echoing Read's argument that affection for a home in western cultures makes the loss of a loved place analogous to the painful loss of a loved person. Read's ideas are an exemplary counterpoint to the experiences presented in this book. He studied people who were deeply rooted in a place they called 'home' and thus experienced profound loss and disorientation when that place vanished. In contrast, the participants I interviewed often describe a sort of rootlessness, a paradoxical attraction towards the wide world mingled with a forlorn yearning for home, underpinned in some cases by the absence of *ever* having felt at home anywhere.

Zita Weber worked with Hungarian refugees in Australia. In the words of one of Weber's respondents, 'We'd gained so much – and yet, we'd lost even more'[4] Though Weber's study was not of voluntary migrants, she does point out the crucial therapeutic value of being able to tell one's story. Weber's migrants had taken the opportunity to talk about their lives and thereby experienced 'important ways of finding coherence and meaning, which act to offset the feeling of dispossession'. The participants in my research also confirmed the importance of 'telling one's story', and the possibility that the story changes in the telling.

There is a problematic sense of the term 'voluntary' in voluntary migration. The question arises frequently for the participants: 'Did I have a choice? Could I have stayed?' The experience of 'existential migration' introduces *degrees of choice* and can invert other common understandings of migration. Whilst many researchers assert that migration results in an uncomfortable discrepancy between inner and outer worlds, for the 'existential migrant' this alteration in the outer environment may paradoxically lessen the discrepancy between inner and outer. For example, some participants in the present study report travelling to a totally foreign and unfamiliar place, turning a corner

---

4. Weber, 2000: 9

and gazing upon a scene that evokes for them a powerful feeling of 'being-at-home' though they have never previously set eyes upon the place. This demonstrates that stories of 'voluntary migration' can reveal assumptions in basic concepts such as 'inner' and 'outer', including what constitutes 'a discrepancy' or 'a similarity'.

June Huntington argues that migration is a distinct and potent category of bereavement. It involves loss of our usual 'life space' and our assumptions about reality,

> ...our model of man, the assumptions we have about human nature ... All these assumptions emerge out of a given time and place; they do not magically appear from nowhere... When our external world (a society that is usually place-time specific) changes, we face a crisis for our assumptive world no longer fits that of the people around us. Inner and outer reality are [sic], temporarily, discordant. Now this is a familiar experience to many of us when we go abroad on holidays. Then we may experience it as exciting, stimulating, lots of fun – though not for everyone of course. But on holiday we know the discrepancy will be temporary and that we choose to return home again where there is a closer fit between inner and outer realities[5].

This typifies the near-invisibility of the voluntary migrant and his or her experience of *not* conforming to the assumptions inherent in the original environment, and their subsequent choice not to return 'home' from the unfamiliar place. Huntington's suggestion that the fit between inner and outer reality is important leads to her assumption that this fit consists of finding an 'outer' world that is *similar enough* to the original world we carry 'inside' of us. Unlike most researchers, Huntington does touch briefly upon the specific experience of the voluntary migrant though it is somewhat dismissed as a minority view and one that does not illustrate her concept of 'place bereavement'.

> Some people, of course, are opened up by such an experience and led to question the external reality of the home environment. Indeed, we all know of people (holidaymakers or migrants) who on arriving at the new place experience a kind of instant recognition, almost a falling in love, an amazing sense of fit between their own inner world and this new external world. These

---

5. Huntington, 1981: 3-4

are often people who have never really felt at home in their own society ... But I believe they are a minority. For most people, the major migratory move from the known to the unknown brings an experience rather like hearing a discordant note in a familiar piece of music (italics added).

Huntington taps but does not open. Her comments provoke engaging questions which she does not pursue but which this book sets out to explore. For example, why does this minority of the population have the experience of not feeling 'at home' in the original homeworld? What constitutes this minority's deep affinity with a foreign culture while their compatriots feel a certain degree of dissonance and a desire to return home to the familiar? Huntington's interest is in exploring the majority experience, as she conceptualizes it, while I endeavour to offer a description of the minority position and its capacity to contravene routine assumptions, offering innovative insights into what constitutes a sense of 'home'.

Huntington points to psychoanalysis; 'For Bowlby, separation trauma and anxiety are greatest when two factors are present: the *presence* of the strange in the *absence* of the loved and familiar'. Migration to an unfamiliar culture involves both of these, and Huntington explicates why *some* people exhibit compulsive attachments to the place-culture milieu of their 'home', displaying apprehension when the familiar is replaced by the threatening foreign world. Bowlby's theory emphasizes the child's primary care-giver as the source of the child's experience of 'containment', supplying a secure base from which to venture forth and test out his or her independence, and to return to for security and sustenance. However, this book attempts to maintain an exploration of the deeper existential realm of this phenomenon, avoiding the instigation of another array of general theories of pathology. An overview of the complexities of the experience of *not* feeling at home may illuminate what it means *to* feel at home. Both Freud and the German philosopher Martin Heidegger referred to the experience of 'the uncanny' or 'unheimlich', the potential for a human to feel not-at-home in the world. Below I will outline their differing perspectives.

CHAPTER 3
THE DEPTH OF THE QUESTION

Based upon Freud's essay '*The Uncanny*' in 1919, the uncanny (unheimlich) is related to what is frightening, especially to what evokes dread and horror. In particular, Freud says the uncanny is that class of frightening experiences which refers back to what was long familiar. Freud struggles with the phenomenon, indicating the paradox that the familiar can also elicit the uncanny while the novel can at times almost be welcoming (for example in travel). The definitions of heimlich (being-at-home) and unheimlich (uncanny) are thus not totally opposite, but also intertwined. For example, Freud's analysis culminates in his assertion that the heimlich can mean both what is familiar and agreeable, and also what is concealed and kept hidden. There is an interesting implication here that *feeling at home entails keeping some things hidden* – we shall see that Heidegger's description of the unheimlich echoes this theme. The experience of the unheimlich occurs when something that should stay hidden in order to feel at home, becomes revealed.

For the purposes of our discussion here, Freud associates the uncanny with those frightening things that we have repressed but that now *recur*, so this uncanny is not something new, but something long familiar that has been pushed out of awareness and then resurfaces momentarily. Our mortality is perhaps the best example of a familiar 'given' which can evoke this feeling of strangeness. Like Heidegger, Freud suggests that anxiety leads to the sense of the uncanny or the unheimlich. But for Heidegger anxiety is an existential, and the unheimlich is an aspect of human being. From 'the unheimlich', Freud generalizes to psychological experiences of 'the unfamiliar' and Heidegger to human 'not being at home' in the world. Later it will be evident that the research seems more consistent with Heidegger's view.

Two psychoanalysts, Grinberg and Grinberg, wrote a book *Psychoanalytic Perspectives on Migration and Exile* and this still remains the major psychoanalytic study of the psychology of emigration and exile, demonstrating how little has been written in this area. The Grinbergs' work includes few references to the subgroup of voluntary migrants who left home by choice, but then always from a perspective that is heavily pre-laden with Freud's theories.

Grinberg and Grinberg fulfil the stereotype of psychoanalyst obsession with childhood sexuality and associate homesickness with unresolved childhood conflicts with the mother. The authors also cite the analyst Balint, who coined the term 'ocnophilic' to refer to the tendency to hold onto what is certain and stable, and 'philobatic' to refer to the tendency to seek out new and exciting experiences and situations. Voluntary migrants are presumed to exhibit the second tendency. I expected that this hypothesis might be confirmed in my own research, however the transcripts suggest that voluntary migrants, perhaps like all of us, exhibit both tendencies, though in specific and idiosyncratic ways. In fact, an ambivalent longing for home *combined with* the attraction to the foreign arises as an essential feature of 'existential' migration. By conceiving of these ambiguities as existential attributes rather than psychological pathology, we accept that they can be *explored* (thus learning something about being human) but not *resolved*, and certainly not 'cured'.

As an illustration of working with migrants at philosophical depth, I present the following brief account. While working with international students at a London university, I met a 26 year-old American postgraduate student who was, for various reasons, having difficulty adjusting to life in London. In our sessions we discussed his previous experiences of living away from home, his experiences of returning home on visits, and his original motivation for leaving America to live as a foreigner in Africa. We discovered that he had always, even as an adolescent, known that he wanted to leave home. His relationships with his family may have been significant in this, and the fact that he was adopted may also have been contributory, though he did not identify it as such. His circumstances and outlook could be assumed to fit aspects of the psychoanalytic diagnosis of 'philobat'. However, *his* experience was that at home he felt 'panic' about the 'nothingness' of the lives and the world he encountered there. He *needed to* 'flee'. In the session where this relationship to nothingness came to light, the client exclaimed 'this feels really philosophical' and he left with a new understanding of the deeper significance of his choices as well as new questions regarding his future plans and a new feeling of ease regarding his contact with 'home' and family. If we had accepted psychoanalytic premises (many of which are now common parlance) our encounter would likely have contracted to examination of his adoption and infant care-giving relationships. This may have lead to important and useful metaphors for the client, but not likely resulting in the philosophical insight he found through our mutual attempts at open exploration.

This philosophical realm is present in the writings of the German existential philosopher, Martin Heidegger. He describes humans as drifting along groundless in life but the anxiety of this drifting is concealed by our self-assured everyday interpretations of life[6]. As long as we can remain convinced by the taken-for-granted appearance of life, we create the impression of ground, covering over the uncanniness

---

6. This section is based on references to 'the uncanny' and 'unheimlich' in Martin Heidegger's main work *Being and Time*, Joan Stambaugh trans,1996.

of existence. This analysis places uncanniness as the primordial fact of our being rather than as a developmental pathology. It is not about mothers not getting along with children but about the structure of human life itself. It is a phenomenon toward which *we all* must respond somehow.

We mostly live according to the familiar publicly accepted conventions. These offer us a 'tranquillized self-assurance', a feeling of being-at-home, in which life is obvious, unremarkable, and taken-for-granted. However, during the course of life, anxiety inevitably arises and this evokes an 'uncanny feeling', a recognition of our precarious gliding atop of nothingness and nowhere. Through anxiety, a person finds him or herself standing out from the familiar, entering the truth of *not-being-at-home*. According to Heidegger, the half-stupor of the conventional and familiar is evident in the consumerist modern world that offers an extensive inventory of prepackaged opportunities to cushion the experience of uncanniness when it emerges unbidden during daily life. Most of these responses aim to return the individual to the comfort of anaesthetized tranquillity. In contrast, it turns out that 'existential migration' could be seen as an expression of this uncanniness rather than simply a fleeing from it. One possibility is that some people may choose to leave what's familiar because the available modes of tranquilization do not convince these individuals that life *is* as it appears, straightforward and meaningful. However, as well as scepticism regarding the conventional, participants also express desires to leave home in order to discover who they *really* are and to fulfil their potential, which reiterates Heidegger's suggestion that uncanniness confronts the individual with the nothingness of the world in which he or she feels compelled to fulfil his or her own self.

What relevance could Heidegger's thought have for those who choose to leave home for the foreign and unknown? We have yet to see if the 'existential migrant' is an existential 'hero' or if he or she is hopelessly lost in the dilemmas of human life, unable to commit to any response.

Does the search for strangeness in the foreign experience, both attractive and unsettling, sustain a way of being that is sensitive to the call for authentic living?

The stories of leaving home depicted here express a felt yearning to leave, a call to go out into the world – perhaps anticipating a resolution that always remains elusive. Are voluntary migrants, like myself, trying to reduce homelessness to the ordinary, temporarily conquering it? Is experiencing homelessness really a longing for home? Perhaps aspects of this longing can be expressed in many ways, metaphorically or concretely, perhaps by buying and settling a 'home' to leaving 'home' altogether.

> Is it a given of the human condition to experience a longing for something not quite within our grasp, call it home, God, the uncanny? A disclosing of Being, as an emerging into the light which brings us closer to others, the Other and ultimately ourselves[7].

It is now my contention that a subset of voluntary migrants engage in such a process of 'existential migration', and thus grapple, either originally or as an unintended consequence of their relocation, with an expression of the deep issues outlined above. By collecting these stories of leaving, experiences of the unfamiliar, feelings of 'home' and self-discovery, I believe that this book addresses us all by acknowledging an aspect of being human that we tend to avoid. The new concept 'existential migration' must at some level tell us something about ourselves not matter who we are.

---

7. Pictet, 2001:45

CHAPTER 4
PREPARING TO LISTEN

The following book is based upon the analysis of in-depth interviews with voluntary migrants[8]. This analysis attempts to ground speculation and theories regarding voluntary migration in actual personal accounts. After describing common features of what I come to call 'existential migration', the book will explore how the present approach contributes something novel to conventional psychologies of migration. Finally, practical implications of the research will be discussed, including applications in the fields of migration studies, psychology of globalization, psychotherapy and counselling, travel and tourism, working abroad, and so on. Since it's a new concept, you will likely come up with your own applications of 'existential migration'.

It is interesting to note that there was no difficulty in recruiting for this study. In fact there were so many migrants interested in being interviewed that the notices requesting volunteers had to be removed shortly after being displayed. The popularity of the topic certainly suggests that there is an unmet need regarding this whole arena of intercultural migratory experience. The majority of participants were

---

8. A 'migrant' has moved from one culture to another where the second is *experienced as* significantly different from the first and for a sufficient duration that the person engages in daily activities and is challenged to undergo some adjustment to the new place.

in their mid thirties to forties and their original home countries included the United Kingdom, Germany, Holland, the former Yugoslavian states, Australia, Greece, Poland, Ireland, the United States, Argentina, Columbia, Latvia, Sri Lanka, and France. This information is provided for interest only, as there was no assumption, nor later indication, that gender, age, or originating culture had any *significant* impact upon what emerged. All identifying information, including country of origin, was deleted or disguised in the book to protect participant confidentiality. Also I think this makes it easier for the reader to read their own life experiences into a story that isn't too identified with the features of another person's life.

As I approached the first interview my growing uncertainty reminded me that the research topic had originated solely from my own personal experiences of cross-cultural relocations. In the opening few minutes I might discover that my questions were purely autobiographical and did not have any resonance for other voluntary migrants. So the first interview was a myriad of anxiety for my first interviewee and for myself. After an initial discussion, I asked 'Nina' the opening question ('Can you tell me about the circumstances of your leaving home?'), ambiguous and ephemeral as it was, and sensed my growing excitement when she responded with little hesitation,

> Um, yes, I've been thinking about this question. I always thought the reason I left home was because I didn't get space to develop myself in the context of my home. I had to; I was expected to be a certain way. But if I think back, it probably was more, I never really felt at home in my birthplace…

Nina's response encouraged me that the lived experience of leaving home was a continuing concern for at least *some* other people, not only me. It suggested that motivations for leaving might be informed by a need for personal space, impinging expectations, and a ubiquitous sense of not really feeling at home in the original 'home'. These were all issues that had resonance for me, and eventually were to be confirmed repeatedly by other participants. Moreover, by the third interview

I felt confident that an unexplored mystery was unfolding; patterns and themes and dilemmas, most of which I could relate to personally though many of which I had not previously elucidated for myself, began to emerge. That long-incubated embryonic sense that began to stalk my awareness during those two weeks in India and Nepal was being substantiated. There was indeed *something* unfathomable and inherent within this process of leaving home; a mystery revealed in the first instance only by its capacity to provoke profound and conflicting emotional responses.

The fact that I am also a voluntary migrant, evident in my Canadian accent, was commented upon as 'helpful' in encouraging people to tell their stories because of the assumption that I would be able to understand their experiences since I also had left. Many participants expressed their reluctance to reveal formative aspects of their experiences of leaving and their on-going predicaments regarding 'home' to anyone who hadn't had a similar life experience.

Participants typically began their interview by talking about the first time they left home, for example leaving for university. They then proceeded to sketch their subsequent comings and goings to the present. During the interview there was also a migration, the movement in the participant's self-understanding. This was evident when the initial question was asked again (with the addition of one word) about half-way through the interview, 'why do you think you left home, *really*?' In response to this second asking, Eva, like many participants, exhibits an emotional shift that many participants experienced, a shift from recounting superficial biographical details to haltingly presenting the unknown edge of more personally experienced urges,

> Well, maybe I've been giving kind of an intellectual answer so far. There was something going on, as I said, on this less articulated level. As I think about it now and knowing myself the way I do now, knowing something about myself that I didn't know then, I think I was compensating. I was compensating for the lack of something. I'm not really sure what that something is, but I felt deficient in some way, very separate from the world of others, disconnected.

> I was missing that connection that would make my being with other people meaningful to me ...

Or another response, from Peter, when asked why he feels he left home, *really*:

> I think I would have gone mad (Laughs). I can't imagine not, I don't know. I think I always imagined it would happen, I go back to the village and I'd drop in and see people who'd just stayed there, and stayed in that village and they've all lived there, I never, ever, ever thought that I would do that, ever! I always thought that I would leave at some point. Partly it was beyond my choice really, it was just inevitable.

The second question of the interview concerns an overall review of the time since leaving home, 'When you reflect upon the time since leaving home, what's it been like for you?' Participants often used this portion of the interview to convey, in some detail, their various experiences, usually highlighting the depth of the pain of leaving and being away as well as the immensely positive aspects of their choice. For example, Peter's response to being asked how it's been for him since leaving:

> Much happier (Laughs.). So much happier, and it's what I always fantasized about, I supposed, as a forlorn child or a teenager, that when I grew up it will be better, I will be freer ... As a child I just thought I needed to be much more independent from them.

Other responses incorporate descriptions of positive aspects of leaving while also acknowledging intricate and subtle indicators of loss, for example, Renata:

> I think there are a lot of payoffs to leaving, but not having home is difficult, although I feel comfortable here in the big city because I'm in the company of strangers, and I'm a stranger myself. But then on the other hand, there is this whole element you can take for granted when you are at home, and which functions without you having to do anything about it ... I think it's about having this network of friends, family, relatives, all this army of people you met throughout your childhood and school years and university years, which existed even if you haven't really been in contact with them. Knowing that they aren't around you is sometimes quite difficult. Not that I want constant

communication, but just that feeling of being part of something.

In these responses we see evidence of the positive aspects of leaving as well as a sense of loss. Some participants really emphasized the difficult experiences since leaving, for example, regret and loneliness. Though interestingly even these participants would make the same choice again, for example Inez:

> At times I've felt I wanted to go back, it's not easy for me to live here. And it makes me realize that people have loved me, but I don't think I will go back. I can't cope with it there, I just can't.

In Inez's response we hear some of the tragic experience of being 'caught' between the difficult decision to leave home and live in a foreign place, and the perceived impossibility of return. The emotional intensity of recognizing the life left behind, unlived, was usually combined with a sense of exile. The second part of that question 'Do you think about returning home?' was designed to gauge where the person was in reference, not only to their original decision to leave, but also in terms of their imagined future. Again, the responses were diverse and unexpectedly emotional. Without exception each participant had given this substantial thought, with some having unsuccessfully attempted to return, some imagining a return or in the process of navigating their return, while for others it was clear they would never go back. But for everyone it was an issue, for some even a *threat*. Below are a few responses to the question 'Do you think about returning home?'

> Sarah – Yeah. A lot. Short term (we laugh knowingly)... But then again if you said to me you'd be living in London for the next ten years, I'd baulk at that as well, I wouldn't want that either. I still hold this image of being a perpetual traveller ... The other thing that comes up that I've been thinking of is that England is more complicated, a more complicated culture. And sometimes if I went home, that would be easy and wonderful, but there's something wrong with easy and wonderful... So anyway, I have this image that every now and then I think of the sunset and twilight and a beautiful sunny day on the beach, and the water, and the people, you know, a wonderful sensuous place. Something about that's easy, and life's got to be complicated, tough.

Graciella – ... that's my question for the last ten years. That's *my* question: My calling, my mantra. It's always there but I try not to think about it (silence) ... I think it would be really nice to have someone who can speak the same language, tell me the same things my father used to tell me, or I could tell him the words my mother used to tell me when I was little.

Marta - Hmmm. I bet everybody cries here? I bet everybody cries at this, do they? But now I feel I couldn't do that to myself again. Who would I be now? I don't even properly speak the language anymore (emotional). It's a nice life there but it's lost to me now.

The last question, 'What does it feel like for you to talk about these things?' elicited some of the most revealing information regarding the depth of feeling around the topic of leaving home. This depth seems to challenge the more cursory accounts of voluntary migration in the literature, where it is suggested that choosing to leave is unproblematic at least in comparison to other forms of migration. Also, these responses overtly attest to the positive impact of having the opportunity to discuss what has remained for most a solitary choice, with little or no affirmation of its personal, and I would argue existential, profundity. It seems to suggest that there is a role for therapeutic sessions incorporating exploration of the experiences of 'existential migration'. Below I offer a number of interviewee samples exemplifying responses to the question, 'What does it feel like for you to talk about these things?'

Sarah – I think about it all the time actually. I do feel quite shaky and quite raw, quite unstable but not in a dramatic way. Sometimes I feel very alienated here, I think (laughs) ...I'm in exile... I feel like I might go and bawl my eyes out now.

Eva – Um, well it's quite inspiring. I feel it is initiating something and it wasn't until I started talking and reflecting on my reasons for leaving that it's come together for me. So, I feel excited because I have realized new insights about myself. I feel very comfortable but there is some emotion underneath. I feel that in the middle of my body, but no tension. A kind of vibrating in a very gentle way, like the sea on a hot day, yes. No big waves.

Martin – It's quite interesting to talk about it from this point of view, because actually I have never focused on leaving home as such ... so it's very, it's not just interesting it's actually made some new connections for me. I think we've managed to go quite deep, probably in some sense as deep as I could go at the moment. It feels a bit loaded the whole thing, but it's good to talk about it, good to think about it and sort of get more of the whole picture.

Inez - I never had the opportunity to put all this together, especially the circumstances, the transition, because that's one of my issues. The language of transition is never spoken, this language to express the sudden shift from one place to another. It's impossible to put into language I suppose ... I think you manage very well to get to the point, to the core of my experience. It's not easy to talk about this. I learned many things and I want to thank you for that.

Peter – It's nice to really talk about it in a sort of condensed period of time, you know the year, and the dates, the chronological order, about various themes and issues. I don't often have a chance to sit down and talk about things in such depth. It is sad but that's OK, I don't find it upsetting but I don't find it joyous either; I find it a fascinating conversation. I find it quite emotional.

Marta – It feels great. It feels overwhelming (emotional) but it also feels liberating. It makes me wonder why I haven't thought some of these things before? It actually feels much better. Yes, it's soothing actually.

Carl – There was a time earlier on when I was trying to say something and all that was actually coming up was emotion, it was quite powerful. Yes, it's painful, that's the best way to put it. I find it awfully painful and there are times when I do cry about it.

CHAPTER 5
THE BUDAPEST MONTHS

The investigation leading to this book began during my trip to Calcutta and Kathmandu. However, the fuller context for this study includes the fact that for over eighteen years I have continued to live in a foreign land. And although I am thereby sensitive to issues of migration and home, many of the participants I interviewed spent time recounting their *original* home-leaving, arriving in a foreign land where many of them had little command of the language and did not understand the social codes. Apart from a year in Oslo in the mid-80s, I had no extensive experience of negotiating a non English-speaking culture. In addition, after 18 years my original confrontation with the new and confusing social codes of a foreign culture has been subsumed within now subtler mixes of familiarity and unfamiliarity. Therefore, I felt I needed to rekindle those initial feelings of arrival and decided that it would be a powerful sensitizing project for me to throw myself into that process of 'acculturation' while simultaneously immersing myself in trying to understand the participants' descriptions of that same process. Of course a temporary sabbatical, with the certainty of return, is radically different from immigrating to a foreign land with prospects of staying there indefinitely. In spite of this, I decided to move to Budapest for four months and as a result I actually did live through a microcosm of the experience of initial arrival in a foreign land. I suspect if I had moved to Budapest open-ended, with the prospect of settling there, these initial feelings would not have been much different, just more intense. Of course it matters that from the beginning I knew there was an end in sight.

I arranged to live in an apartment in the centre of Budapest for four months while working intensely on the analysis of the interviews and research write-ups. I had never been to Budapest and could not speak a word of Hungarian, which I was assured was an especially impenetrable language. I knew no one in the city, except to a perfunctory extent the couple I was subletting from, who kindly oriented me during my first three days there. After that, I was alone – with a booklet of public transit tickets, some information about the famous local baths, and a city map. As anticipated, it was a powerful experience.

While in Budapest I intended to keep a record of my day-to-day life and encounters and to some extent I accomplished that. The fact that I often felt resistant to writing in the diary was itself significant, though the first entries were actually made even before I left London. As I sat down to fulfil this commitment to record the process of living in Hungary, I became increasingly aware of this reluctance to record what was happening. I felt hesitant about bringing something more fully into awareness, especially in the context of my isolation. This reluctance on my part made me consider that perhaps for others too there was a need to maintain distance from difficult feelings and thus a tendency towards silence when arriving in a new land. Perhaps without a promise of shared understanding, it is too intense to reflect upon or speak about difficulties that revolve around such primordial issues as the loneliness and *shame* of self-imposed exile.

The process of 'migrating' began at least four weeks prior to my planned departure. This is reminiscent of the descriptions by participants, one of whom packed her bags a month before leaving home and left them in full view beside the front door. Experientially, migration begins long before leaving home. While finishing off my work in London I already formed a firm image of what my Budapest apartment would look like though I had never seen a photo of it. I tried to vary the image so as not to be too shocked or disappointed when the reality turned out to diverge greatly, perhaps depressingly, from the fantasy. I also found myself imagining a whole new life there, an opportunity for a different way of living. It was a new beginning and *everything* would be different. I would be different. Counter-balancing this positive anticipation were darker prospects: I would become isolated, afraid, unproductive, sinking into an internal turmoil. I won't understand the language, which will accentuate my exclusion. I began to panic that my fantasized refuge and 'home' for my exciting new life would be inhospitable and cold to the touch. These perennial hopes and simmering fears reveal that major themes in my life were already active in anticipation. A whole imagined world was slowly being populated, giving me *something* to respond to rather than the radical emptiness and complete uncertainty of the unknown foreign place. So I left for Budapest with a feeling for what it would be like to live there, packed with scenes that I had already 'lived' in preparation. I arrived with memories of a place where I had never set foot. My first evening in Budapest I wrote,

> Walking around the city I feel the excitement of a new place, already trying to make it familiar, while also already rejecting it. The buildings are not pretty enough, the place smells of third world diesel, the people are too attractive or not attractive enough, the apartment is too small or too big, too quiet and claustrophobic or too public, noisy, and intrusive. Looking forward to being on my own but also afraid I'll spiral down into a dark isolation and become a zombie walking the streets, unable to touch or be touched by the sensual world. This city is grand but faded, an imperial capital in need of a good dusting.

In this first entry there is a palpable expression of the ambiguity, and the true polarity of voluntary migration. Choice becomes agonizing doubt coupled with accusatory responsibility. As you will see, my experience closely parallels the stories of many of the participants and so reinforces the sense that moving to Budapest during the analysis did sensitize me to the intricacies of what I had heard in the interviews.

My mood during those first few days was characterized by both optimism and sorrow. I was finding it difficult to slow down and be with my experience, like there was nowhere safe enough, no corner deep or dark enough where I dare let my attention leave the surface world for the inner world of meaningful connection and bodily feeling. By the third evening the scales of ambivalence had tipped slightly. I felt more excitement but also more longing for an anchor in terms of something or someone familiar.

> I have just gone for my first Hungarian beer in a local tavern frequented by a friendly student crowd. I am beginning to feel that I can find a way to be here, but still this opaque image of myself as a ghost on the edge of the crowd, not really here, or not really seen, not able to break into the Hungarian world because of the language that surrounds them and excludes me. I didn't speak to anyone all evening and awkwardly ordered my beer using sign language. Physically I feel like my body is weak, it doesn't know how to be strong here, or that it's not allowed for me to feel strong and centred without appearing arrogant. A strong foreigner is a despised foreigner. I find myself pining for friends, that having another human with me, a little world in English, would make *everything* possible, perhaps even motivating me to learn the few words that I will certainly need to survive here for these months. And how crazy that I should already want the company of the people I happily left only 2 days ago – people I was so willing to abandon for blissful solitude.

It is at this point that I commence the task that had brought me to this city. I set up my computer and begin to organize my work on the interview transcripts. I realize quickly that it is 'a very eerie experience' reading others' accounts of settling in a strange land while I am doing exactly the same thing. Even the simplest daily tasks, shopping, banking, taking a tram, are consciously reviewed as to how they can be accomplished without words. The signage along the city streets provide me with few clues as to what lies behind each shop door and 'today's menu' is a complete mystery. I find myself intrigued and exhausted, vacillating between my refuge in the courtyard apartment and the attraction and excitement of the alien environs waiting to envelop me.

Strange experience working on the research, being possessed one after another by the people I've interviewed. Sometimes feeling they are describing my exact experience as I sit here in this lonely city with its sad history. I think it's an amalgamation of my own solitude resonating with their narratives, intensified by the potent airless space of the two-room apartment. I am reluctant to engage with being here, feeling like I don't want to learn the language and feeling ashamed and guilty about that, feeling that I don't want to leave the room and having to push myself to go out and meet people. Total ambivalence; attracted and indifferent to being here, while now imagining the London I had grown tired of as a city of promise, pregnant with possibilities for connecting with people and pursuing life.

By the second week I was feeling more excited but also drained by the work and living; it was too seamless. I was waking up early in the morning with a feeling of simmering resentment. Something in me felt maimed, hobbled, unable to reach full throttle, and this feeling comes tinged with a tendency to blame others (Hungarians, the world). I was having vivid dreams, with themes of loss, regret, inconsolable sorrow that also strangely brought a sense of relief. I felt I was descending into a vigorous internal world populated only by me and these disembodied interviews, locked in a mutually reinforcing echo of homelessness and solitude.

Both my dreams and my waking desires constantly reinforced the importance of relationship in my life. I had by now at least encountered some fellow foreigners out in taverns. I found it odd how we foreigners gravitated to each other, complicit in our marginality, and how our conversations were a mix of our own statelessness combined with subtle criticisms of local culture. On these occasions I was left wondering if our dislocation conjures a feeling of inferiority that we compensate for by disparaging the belonging enjoyed by the locals around us. As I neared the end of my three-month stay, I wrote the following in my diary, feeling nostalgic and lyrical at the thought of leaving,

It is another beautiful warm evening. I noticed as I started to walk across the bridge that there were more people than usual wandering around, kind of a festive atmosphere I thought, perhaps a boat has just moored and the passengers are disembarking and making their way back to the nearest tram stop. I walked down through the park where I usually sit listening to a local band with the grandmothers in the afternoon. It was nice being by the river, cooled by its breeze after the stifling city heat of the past few weeks. I bought a large bottle of beer and as I walked back I gazed upon the usual sites; the faded yellow tram (number 6) crossing the bridge, the dark shadows of Margaret Island, the fairyland castle and parliament buildings lighting the riverbank and the dark hills in the distance. I will miss this place, and I know already I'll romanticize it far beyond reality.

I had imbued a degree of sustenance from the mutual recognition that had developed between the local shopkeepers and myself. They greeted me, laughed at my attempts to speak in Hungarian and seemed to enjoy our charade-based communication. Their recognition made me feel real. I became tangible. I eventually formed some familiarity with a circuit of town that stretched from the Danube to the ring road, and I walked it every day in order to feel some sense of mastery over something. When it came time to leave Hungary I was deeply sad. Synchronistically, my departure coincided with the Hungarian national day of celebration. From early morning there was the deafening sound of fighter jets strafing the Danube, mixed with music from loudspeakers, and massive crowds walking down to the river's edge. My small leaving, unbeknownst to anyone, was juxtaposed with such a massive shared event. I couldn't shake the feeling that I wanted to say goodbye to people I couldn't even have said hello to; local shopkeepers, the helpful staff in the DVD rental shop, the waitress at the Blue Tomato.... As I left it came to me that living in this strange place was like feeling both ends of a magnet at once – the irresistible pull at one end and the invisible repulsion at the other. To this day I have not returned to Budapest. The prospect excites and frightens me, like I'd be breaking some natural law. Waiting for my plane I wrote these final few whimsical lines,

> The world calls us to bring it to life. It needs human being to lift it to its feet, and simultaneously we live in order to lift the world, we need each other. When

the call of the world and the respondent human 'match', a feeling of seeking is satiated and the human feels 'at home', for a moment. But perhaps at times the call can be too strong, or the individual does not respond, generating a feeling of invalidation. There is a basic desire for completion, from self and world, to connect and flow, but these moments that allow us to genuinely feel 'at home' are transitory and fragile. Home is a human aspiration.

CHAPTER 6
THEMES OF EXISTENTIAL MIGRATION

These accounts of leaving home are grouped according to the most common themes that, all in all, depict the experience of existential migration. Hopefully there is enough of the living voice remaining here to open a response in the reader, to lure the reader into feeling 'possessed' by these experiences, just as I felt in that apartment in central Budapest. These stories offer complex and mysterious feelings without fixed and settled conclusions.

> It is in this writerly space where there reigns the ultimate incomprehensibility of things, the unfathomable infiniteness of their being, the uncanny rumble of existence itself… Various philosophers have described this uncanniness as the realm of the *il-y-a* in Levinas, the *es gibt* in Heidegger, *wild being* in Merleau-Ponty, the *Real* in Lacan, or the *khora* in Derrida – it is the frightful allure of Existence itself that fascinates the writer and the artist but that cannot be spoken. Levinas describes *il-y-a* as something that resembles what one hears when holding an empty seashell against one's ear … As if the emptiness is full, as if the silence is a murmuring, as if one hears the silent whisper of *the Real*.

The following descriptions are pooled narratives of existential migration, composites of actual accounts. Hopefully by reading what follows, even those who have not embarked upon 'existential migration' will form a felt sense of this process - a feeling that is itself an understanding.

---

9. van Manen, 2002: 243

6.1　WHO AM I?

The stories of existential migration depict *something* within pulling the person forward, something that demands to be lived out. If we call this something a '*self*', then this self forms as a personal response to our interactions in life. In the interviews, it is clear that a person's environment has a crucial influence on the ability to develop. To a significant extent, the familiar home environment impinges upon one's attempts to let a self unfold in its unique way. Therefore, existential migration can be a 'self' protective act in the sense that leaving constitutes a *search for space* where a self can unfold and respond more freely. Half of the voluntary migrants interviewed said they required a combination of space and relationship in order for their sense of self to develop, reminiscent of a respectful relationship with a good therapist.

There is an onus on the person to protect the uniqueness of their own self. From early life many participants recognize their 'difference' and the dawning realization that their personal attributes and sensitivities are uncommon. Being aware of one's difference can generate a life trajectory distinct from conventionally prescribed life courses resulting in ever-increasing distance between oneself, the development of peers and the expectations of the *available* world. Along with this distance is a heightened sensitivity to self-and-other interaction. One is set apart as having a different identity, in some sense a less naïve one, as though something, life events, inherent sensitivities, caused one to grow up too fast, see too much, loose an innocent belief in the taken-for-granted presentation of things. Sensing this, such individuals compare themselves to others in an attempt to assess their own belonging.

There seems to be a paradoxical relationship with the world in which the world poses as a threatening influence on the developing self while also offering the only possibility of its development. One's nascent identity needs to be kept safe from being swamped and contaminated by conventional expectation, but simultaneously that identity needs to linger in relationship with others in order to develop at all. No one develops in isolation.

There is a tension in trying to belong somehow while also needing the space to protect one's fledgling identity from the implosion of the familiar. To safeguard one's unique potential. The converse of this dynamic comes alive in a foreign environment where the distance from 'home' makes it feel safe to acknowledge a degree of commonality with the home culture without drowning in the sea of sameness all around. I am free to be Canadian when I'm living in Europe but it's too threatening to identify as Canadian in the 'home" environment of Canada.

One strategy for protecting the emerging self is to build up psychologically defensive layers between self and environment. However, this leads to isolation (as opposed to independence, which is relational), and if we become too isolated we lose the interpersonal element in self-formation. One of the participants, Patricia, described her lack of relationship to other people as threatening her connection to existence itself. If anyone caught sight of her in her state of disconnection they would see how fundamentally she lacked a sense of belonging. Some participants felt their existence was like a precarious balance between the two extremes of being imploded upon by others and being isolated into disappearance.

In early life and adolescence, Peter had to be cautious about his contact with the world. The world offered disappointment, puzzlement, and rejection, while providing little in the way of protection or support. He found that he had to 'close down' in early life, when escape was not an option, and only when he left home was he able to contemplate a more open re-connection with his environment. He used travel to try to 'shock himself' into connecting to the world again. The total unfamiliarity of foreign places, including extreme or even brutalizing situations, was sought in order to break himself open, 'kick myself alive' as he says, to return to a more fluid relationship with life. Being able to cope with such foreign or difficult experiences was also significant in developing his sense of self-worth. In negotiating the strange world he realized he had worthy characteristics such as independence, the ability to meet others without losing or sacrificing himself and a kind of meditative non-attachment. Once a sense of identity and self-worth begins to take root and self-protection is less necessary, one can engage more and navigate the unfamiliar more freely, in turn bolstering self-worth. This cycle can even lead to the identity of 'migrant as admired other', possessing the characteristics envied by those who remain settled, sedentary out of fear of the unfamiliar. But it is an ironic twist of fate when a struggle to exist is misinterpreted as 'heroic' by the very people who contributed to the necessity for that initial struggle in the first place. They admire the hero that they unknowingly made.

The ubiquitous primordial motif of the 'hero's return'[10] is evoked in many of the accounts given by participants. After a difficult journey of self-discovery and worldly adventure, these individuals express a desire to return home to a welcome that celebrates their achievements and an indication that their struggles and the person they've become is finally respected, even if little understood. To some extent this is a self-protective measure of the type: 'I can be who I really am now that I have world-recognition, they can't pull me back into their pre-formed expectations now that they have to recognize how much I've exceeded them'. Worldliness as a prophylactic against erosion by the conventional. The wide world certainly offers more alternatives than the restricted array of roles available in any locale, especially in more traditional cultures. For example, for a woman from a traditional South American family, returning with an advanced education might result in being respected as a unique sort of woman, self-supporting

---

10. For example, as described by Joseph Campbell in *The Hero with a Thousand Faces* (1949, New York: Pantheon Books)

and financially independent from men. New possibilities exude from a person who's no longer tied to the caprice of the homeworld. The expectations of the home culture aren't so easily imposed when the person who returns is recognized as a mixture of familiar and strange (which in fact, they've always been but it was not previously acknowledged).

Rather than a set identity grown from a specific place, the possibility emerges that living in various cultures offers a more fluid identity, elaborated by the complexity of not quite fitting in anywhere and freedom from having to identify with one fixed place. Camilla notices that while living at home, she was so consumed with the effort to fit in and belong that she could never relax into a feeling of being-at-home. Only after she left for London could Camilla return to her home environment and identify with it in a less restrictive, less crucial way. She had not only developed her own self-confidence while away, but by living in a foreign land she had also come to accept her identity as 'outsider'. Paradoxically, identifying as an outsider and finally meeting others who didn't fit in, seemed to give Camilla the 'belonging' necessary to make it possible to 'choose herself' rather than conform to an imposed self stipulated by a rather oppressive homogeneous environment.

Despite the implication that geographic relocations can be positive in the ways hinted at above, questions about our 'where-ness' apparently remain crucially important. Not knowing *where* to locate can be very unsettling and confusing because it carries the implication of not knowing who one is. The constant question 'where should I be?' can interrupt the task of piecing together a self that feels contiguous, leading to a crisis of identity exacerbated by the need to know 'who should I be?' and 'which life should I lead?' One attempted solution is to try to live more than one life, but this is unsettling and ungrounding, not to mention impossible. For the 'existential migrant' the question of identity is intricately bound up with, and compounded by, the felt need to relocate, to travel, and to leave. And this relocation itself is an expression of how deeply felt is the question of identity.

A contrast to these experiences can be seen in the story of one participant who is dealing with questions of identity arising from being brought to London, his 'adopted' country, as a young child. Kumar grew up in Britain and acknowledges how much his daily identity is British, yet on a deeper level he feels intimately affiliated to his native country. Though he is isolated from the way of life in his original country, for example not knowing the language and customs, this does not lessen the feeling of being uprooted from there, nor the hope that return remains possible. Visiting his ancestral village, Kumar immediately felt a strong emotional connection and a birthright to the family land. This property was a symbolic anchor for his life though he is realistic about how impossible it would be for him to ever re-integrate fully into living there. Kumar enjoys his special status, the exotic and unique aspect associated with having a mixed identity in the UK. Unlike the other participants, Kumar has not heeded a 'call' to venture away from the known to find the mystery of self. His 'problem' is of a different nature – he seems engaged in trying to knead the multiplicities of two cultural stories of himself into the requirements of one life.

From the point of view of those who embark on 'existential migration', to be totally identified with one's own culture can prevent the self from developing and maturing. Total assimilation is stunting in its emphasis on predictability and conformity. Staying in one place can result in being solidified by the environment. Exposure to other cultures lessens restrictions, allowing one to experience various beliefs or views without having to become totally identified with any one. People are always more than the fixed roles societies offer. And for some reason, these particular migrants seek to manifest this 'more'. For such a person, it can be intensely irritating when other people make assumptions about who one is based upon accent, country of origin etc, thereby nullifying one's difficult journey for *self*-definition.

There can be a tense and resentful relationship between the so-called 'existential migrant' and the environment that would seek to simplify him or her into a stereotype.

This section emphasizes that a human 'self' is created through responses to one's surroundings; the environment can either support or obstruct development of one's potential. For some voluntary migrants, the call to realize one's potential overrides most other considerations, including the need to belong. In this sense, leaving home can be a 'self-protective' choice. Moving to a foreign place fosters flexibility to develop oneself according to an 'inner call', something that probably was not encouraged in the home environment. Because the foreign place is different, it offers a chance to examine the home culture from a safe distance, without opening the door to a flood of homogeneity that would obliterate the individual's uniqueness It is difficult to maintain a balance between the threat of implosion and arid isolation. Balance requires a combination of space and relationship that was not experienced in the home culture. For some people there is a desire to return home after achieving a sense of self that is fluid, complex, and able to withstand the pull to conform exhibited in the home environment. At the same time, finding oneself 'rootless' can result in a fragile sense of self that is constantly unsettled, restless, and seeking respite. This discussion of the 'self' underpins the stories of leaving home that follow.

6.2 WHERE DO I BELONG?

Closely linked to the complex issue of identity, and prima facie nearly its opposite, is the question of 'belonging'. Who I feel myself to be is a meaningful reaction to who *they* say I am. This section will describe the duality of belonging, on one hand the warmth and security of intimate human connection, on the other hand the oppressive shadow of conventionality, pressure to conform, and suffocating expectations.

Positive human relationships can ground a person and provide a sense of 'belonging-to'. Participants anticipated that belonging would incorporate the experience of being 'seen', feeling understood and accepted, within the space *to be* without the intrusion of others' expectations. It is the felt sense of being cared about as the person one recognizes oneself to be. However, this ideal belonging was rare in the experiences of the people interviewed. Without a feeling of belonging, a sensation of being rootless and intangible can form; there is a dearth of permanent connections with others.

Voluntary migrants embody incompatible needs; to yearn to belong yet also to *have to* escape the belonging offered because it feels suffocating and entrapping. There is a tension inherent in the desires to belong squashed by the claustrophobia of the implicit impositions and demands of the '*conditional* belonging' offered. This process generates a desperate need to escape, for some it even feels like 'running for one's life'. It is significant to note that often others in the family, for example siblings who inhabit 'the same' environment, don't leave but instead attempt to negotiate conflicts *within* a feeling of being 'at home'. In fact what initially appears to be an invasive environment where no one would flourish, turns out to be more ambiguous and mysterious, and the question eventually focuses again on the individual who left, 'so why did *you* leave?' Rather than examining a troubled individual psyche or a dysfunctional environment, the mystery seems to be located in the *interaction* between a unique individual self and shared surroundings.

During the interviews the statement, 'I never really felt I belonged at home in the first place' became a common refrain within the stories of leaving. For some, as long as they can remember they felt that home was not their place, as Graciella describes it, 'it was where I was *put* to grow up'. For others, there was a specific period in their development when it dawned on them that they could not stay, often because their actual way of being was not understood or not welcome. In the latter situation, usually this person was 'the one' in the family who didn't quite fit in, never *felt* accepted, and always stood slightly apart from the wider sense of community. This experience, especially for a young person, is painful and confusing. In trying to make sense of not fitting in, individuals seem to alternate between explanations grounded in family dynamics (absent father and overprotective mother, but then needing to explain why siblings didn't also leave), and individual sensitivities (I have always valued my independence) in order to explain the motive to detach *self* from the only world available.

Many strategies are employed to try to cope with this confusing and painful predicament. For example, getting along with everyone is one way of trying to feel safe, less isolated and adrift, but paradoxically the strategy of trying to belong everywhere maintains the experience of not really belonging anywhere. This reinforces the assumption that who one *truly* is (behind this disguise of malleability) cannot be accepted by the world one knows. The experience of not-belonging raises fundamental and disquieting questions about the structure of life itself. Some of the participants have found convincing answers in philosophical or spiritual domains (discussed in a later chapter), and for some the experience of never quite belonging has become so familiar as to become a given of their existence. It just is. *Explanations are post hoc.* Not-belonging is the one experience that can be presumed. Such not-belonging is felt and expressed at various levels, in the arms of a parent, in the dynamics of the family home, with peers at school, in the local community, feeling marginal in relation to the cultural values of the nation as a whole. Even at a young age, some participants report identifying more with foreigners and others on the margins of society.

A definition of 'belonging' will emerge gradually in the way this word is actually used by participants in their interviews. Initially, we can say that belonging refers to the felt experience that one is accepted; even one's difference is taken into account and welcomed. In the context of this discussion, 'to belong' suggests being native to, to have a right of habitation, notions of equality and connection rather than feeling superfluous or antagonistic. A very homogenous and conforming culture provides particularly difficult terrain in which to take root. For some inexplicable reason some individuals, who arose from the 'same' earth as their neighbours, stand out as 'different', as not fitting in. It can feel quite hopeless when one is singled out as different and subjected to marginalization, teasing, or even violent rejection, while the actual reason for being alienated in this way cannot be pinpointed. Lest a spurious causal explanation be made, it is important to acknowledge that the experience of difference predates the experience of rejection. Social rejection was not the source of 'difference' but an acknowledgement of it, albeit at times a particularly hurtful one. Even for those participants who remained popular and actively included in their social worlds, the subjective knowledge of their difference seemed to create a second skin, wherein developed an anxious perspective on daily life. For those who cannot cover over or deny their difference, or ingratiate themselves successfully in various peer groups, the environmental response can be rejecting, the consequent message 'different is bad' compounding the difficulties of feeling one does not belong.

Martin's peers labelled him 'different', and bullied him consistently from a young age. He feels that this experience eventually crystallized as a sense of isolation and alienation from his entire culture. Renata says it's obvious that she is a stranger when she's in London, but in her home country it was less obvious that she was also a stranger there. By 'stranger', she means whether a person feels part of the community or not. Although Renata describes herself as sociable, even from a young age she felt apart from rather than a part of the community. She maintained a distance from the group; she remained somewhat disengaged in order to make her own independent choices about who to connect with. This need for space and independence made Renata stand out as different in her home culture. Part of the motivation for leaving home was to find places and people that could welcome her while allowing her to maintain a sense of her own self. Renata, Martin, and other individuals like them seem to have an *innate* openness to something deeper than the mere appearance of life, an openness which is at odds with traditional or homogenous cultures and an openness which these individuals want to protect in themselves, even at the cost of not belonging.

For two participants realizing they were attracted to their own gender later complicated the experience of being different and not fitting in. This creates a powerful combination of two essentially secretive individual processes. The awareness of culturally 'deviant' sexual desires formed within a preexisting atmosphere of difference, creating a secretive shame that only adds to the potency of not belonging[11]. For Peter, the realization that he was attracted to men coincided with feeling alienated, reinforced by teasing at school. This exacerbated his feeling that he was not *of* the place – he felt tense, intimidated, and by grammar school, now in an all-male environment, Peter had withdrawn from almost all interaction. He was left feeling depressed, lonely, and scared, with no significant support at home.

In contrast, Carl experienced his home as a secure world of loving family relations in spite of his atypical tendencies, notably an unusually strong interest (compared to his family) in the external 'wider' world. There had never been any doubt in Carl's mind that he was loved and welcome at home, until he came out as gay. In Carl's experience, he had changed (or more accurately, *revealed* his difference) while the environment had remained the same. Though his religious family said they could 'accept' him, he began to feel not accepted, inferior, and unhappy. The previous assumption of home no longer functioned for him as a gay son and this signified a painful sudden shift from secure belonging to insecure homelessness. Carl felt he had not been

---

11. The process of 'existential migration' has within it an element of secrecy, in large part due to its, until now, lack of pubic recognition. This has more than a passing similarity to the solitary process of sexual 'coming out'.

prepared by his childhood to deal with this schism, and he muses that a difficult childhood might have made it easier to cope with change and to leave. To lose what appeared to be an idyllic childhood and simultaneously acquire a second-class status was traumatic.

Carl's response was to leave his homeland to search for an opportunity to regain a positive experience of home, to relocate where assumptions functioned differently and where he could perhaps foster a sense of balance, meaning, and belonging. This exodus cannot be causally reduced to his coming out, his family dynamic, or the overall oppressive environment. It seems a complex combination of all these circumstances, in interaction with Carl's inherent curiosity and affinity to otherness. Even when he was much younger, Carl always wanted to travel. He often experienced the opposite of homesickness; in his native language this is acknowledged by a term that means 'far-sickness', a craving to go somewhere else far away, away from home. No one was surprised when Carl subsequently announced that he would do voluntary work in Indonesia, and he still periodically re-experiences this desire to go, to seek the space where he can breathe. When he visits home, he experiences a physical feeling of pain as he rediscovers again that this is not home for him. It was a major family trauma when Carl originally left and then worse when he explained to his parents that he would never return. Carl's pain is connected to the experience of returning to the place he remembers as an 'idyllic' (though in a sense illusory) home and knowing he will never belong there again because he can never again be himself there. No one, not even his closest childhood friends, understand when he attempts to explain the depth of his loss.

Inez also found that her burgeoning sexuality served to crystallize her predisposition to marginality. She felt she could not talk to others about the changes she was undergoing in adolescence. It was taboo in her family to discuss sexuality so the physical changes and emerging desires highlighted what she already felt, that she didn't belong in her family, or the wider conservative society. She interpreted her difference as shameful. Feeling different is 'bipolar', both positive and negative, and for Inez the negative manifested when her difference alienated her from a feeling of belonging. Puberty triggered a withdrawal from peers and family because Inez already felt peculiarly marginal, exhibited in her unusual aesthetic pursuits and her pronounced opinions on social justice. At night she began to dream of England, imagining that being isolated and different in a foreign land would be less painful than alienation at home, and in fact these dreams functioned as a secretive private world. Many of the participant narratives reveal that one can feel more lost and alone at home than in the most foreign and unfamiliar places.

A feeling of not-belonging where everything and everyone says one *should* belong can result in a lack of confidence that one will belong anywhere. Camilla felt she had to belong somewhere and being in a marginal position in the family, she looked to the wider culture but the homogeneity of that culture excluded anyone who was not obviously and fundamentally 'the same'. Camilla's foundations were shallow. Her parents were immigrants so in order to really belong she had to disown the foreign aspects of her parent's identities. Sounding the same as others is an important dimension in belonging to the dominant culture; accents are an indication of sameness or difference, so Camilla undertook to cultivate the correct enunciation. Having to manage one's identity in a way that is not natural in order to mimic the sameness of the surrounding culture can result in uncomfortable feelings of being inauthentic, a phoney, fraudulent, of betraying oneself while never quite persuading the group whose acceptance one craves. This can leave a person with a compromised sense of self, further compounding the lack of belonging one was trying to assuage; the person potentially accepted is not even oneself. Camilla felt she had no right to be living in the place she was born. She did not belong to the culture in the same way as others whose families were all interconnected and who could relate to each other in the culturally condoned manner. She felt shunned and desperate. This resulted in a sense that she had no home in the world at all and didn't even belong on earth.

Based upon the interviews, we can see how experiences of not-belonging begin to crystallize around and reinforce latent and murky predispositions towards leaving. For example, from as far back as Ben can remember he always knew he wouldn't stay where he grew up. He had an *innate sense* that he actually needed to get far away from home. Not really belonging to family, social world, peers, or friends, can feel so desperate that leaving the country feels crucial, like a necessary amputation. As mentioned above, missing this human connection in the intimate place where one is born is especially painful. Missing this sense of belonging is not in itself a predictor of 'existential migration' - some who left *did* have a degree of belonging and peer popularity and many who stayed behind presumably did not. We cannot assume that those people who stay at home, or who return home after brief foreign excursions, have an *unshakeable* sense of belonging, but presumably they feel less ambivalent and so perhaps less desperate. Or perhaps they harbour greater fear of the unfamiliar, or they lack the greater need for independence, or their homeworlds have enough diversity that they can find a corner where their not-belonging finds solace ... *somehow* they seem able to find non-geographic ways of coping with inevitable fractures in belonging.

According to Eva even the slightest connection could be reason enough to stay in her country of birth, but without that she felt she had no choice and no dilemma, *she had to go*. She left in search of a place where she could belong and she now sees that as impossible – she is destined to be an outsider everywhere. Marginality becomes a part of one's identity but Eva feels it's possible to achieve some acceptance of this. She has tried to welcome and accept the part of herself that will never belong.

Conformity is required to *fit in* and that can feel like too much of a sacrifice of the personal freedom to choose for oneself. Nina feels it is easier to live in an uncaring, unsupportive, and lonely foreign place to safeguard her freedom and integrity. Conformity means not being honest about one's own feelings or thoughts, in other words, pretending. In her case, independence is valued even more than the warmth of human contact.

On the positive side, leaving for a foreign place can provide the opportunity to reinvent oneself, to be freed from a constraining self-image and become more individualized and less controlled by convention. Not belonging allows a kind of creative jiggle-room between self and environment. The challenge of living in a very foreign place, where there is no familiarity and no foundation for a sense of belonging, can even be experienced as joyful! It offers the chance to begin again, without having to compensate for the 'failure' of not fitting in at home.

The individual who doesn't fit in can also form an attitude of rejection towards the home, either at the level of family, town, or nation. Rita experienced daily life in her hometown as lacking any stimulation and she found it a stifling place to live. It would have felt unbearable to remain in such a provincial and isolated habitat, out of contact with the wider world. Rita's academic interests and liberal political views would have isolated her further in this environment and even now she chooses not to contact people who have stayed in her hometown in order to avoid repeating the experience of being misunderstood and ostracized. The only other choice open to Rita in her home environment would have been to assimilate, censor her difference by adopting nonthreatening and socially tolerated modes of expressing a watered-down dissent. But this was unpalatable. Many of her early friends stayed or have since returned to live where they grew up and Rita perceives them as trapped there. From their perspective, her settled peers perceive Rita as a 'fish out of water' when she visits her own hometown. A fish out of water in the place she was born and raised.

Inez experienced her home society as violent, disturbingly unjust, with attitudes she could not abide. She was disillusioned by the lack of any sincere desire for change, and the overbearing importance of power. She saw no hope of having a meaningful life purpose if she remained in her home culture and she prefers the struggles of her foreign life, though it is suffused with distinct difficulties. Martin experiences his home culture as rigid in terms of norms and expectations. The choice facing him was to abide by these and feel suffocated or to become completely isolated in his own culture. Martin feels that his culture smothered the possibilities for exploring his potential. It is significant to him that his native language does not have a way of talking about enjoying life and he sees this as concomitant with the national mentality, which was always foreign to him. For Martin, life is fundamentally about choice. It is unclear what has allowed Martin, Rita, and Inez to take such a variant stance to their home cultural assumptions but it may be that early experiences of not belonging or peer rejection helped to maintain distance from their surrounding cultures, permitting them to further develop their openness to the world.

Not belonging was also an issue for Kumar, who was brought to the UK at age five by his parents in order to offer him a better life. Though not an instance of *voluntary* migration (or existential migration), Kumar's problematic issues of identity and belonging suggest that some of the aspects described above might generalize to other groups of people. Kumar's experience is that his difference stands out and defines him in each of his national contexts. In his native land he cannot speak the language and would be taken as British, yet back in the UK his race sets him apart. He feels he straddles two worlds and negotiates the divergent values of these two worlds. He feels in part blended into both cultures and simultaneously protruding. He needs both cultures to feel whole but paradoxically doesn't fit into either. This experience leads him to wonder if he'll ever be comfortable anywhere, or ever feel fully at home.

Kumar knows how to conform to the role expected of him in whichever world he's in but there are moments of schism when he's obviously out of place, for example when he realizes he's in a room full of white British. He feels he's been very anglicized and ingrained into the social establishment of British culture while also being a person of colour, and he perceives this as an incongruity. For Kumar, there is a question of not-belonging partly based upon race; something is missing and his search for that missing piece points him towards his original homeland. In his description we see the clear overlap between issues of belonging and identity, and in Kumar's consideration of how to resolve these dilemmas it is hard not to speculate that we are witnessing the birth of a process of existential migration.

As indicated above, the acquiescence to others' expectations, social norms and conventions can be experienced as completely suffocating. There is a tension between resisting expectations and ending up isolated or even rejected, and trying to meet them while losing one's sense of personhood and self-direction. From the point of view of these participants, fitting in and belonging, no matter how prized, implies a hefty sacrifice. It is not uncommon for the individuals interviewed to attempt to resolve this dilemma by residing in two or more locations, for example, having another house in the countryside, or in another country. This provides a place of escape, and though the exact meaning of this remained mysterious, it seems that *dual belonging* may offer an experience of community acceptance while maintaining enough relational distance to allow for independence. For others, a resolution consisted of balancing intrusive belonging with the frequent refuge of solitary travel to foreign places. For most participants it was unthinkable not to have this other place to escape to, or at the very least to have easy access to frequent international travel. However, always going back and forth, between connection and solitude, home and abroad, can make life feel fragmented and lead to a desire to connect everything together in one place. Then again, having everything in one place would compromise the essential ability to choose when to be with others and when to be alone – there would be less opportunity for self-regulation between solitude and being with others, generating those same feelings of panic and suffocation; a vicious circle. It can feel crucial to maintain one's own freedom of choice regarding the demands of relationship.

For Patricia, living alone in an isolated place on the edge of the city offers a solution to this dilemma since others need to make a special journey to visit her. In this case being with people becomes a personal decision, requiring an invitation, no spontaneous 'popping by'. Patricia finds that the transition from solitude to the social world requires time to 'crank herself up'. The more time spent alone the more protective layers build up and the longer it takes to make the transition back into relationship with others. In Patricia's case, she links this experience with her original home environment, where she was not allowed to be alone long enough to dwell in her private inner world without others imposing. At that time, this sense of inner privacy was her escape, her 'other place'. Unlike others in her family, for some reason *Patricia needed this*. Patricia searches for a balance between *wanting* everything in one place and fearing it. In this, Patricia expresses her version of a common theme - the difficulty of reconciling the need for connection, belonging, relationship and the need for solitary respite from those demands. Patricia's siblings do not understand her experience of this dichotomy.

Martin anticipates that emotionally he could not have developed at all if he hadn't left home. If he had to stay, Martin feels he would have literally felt suffocated, describing his experience of suffocation powerfully as feeling like being tied up, restrained, bringing a physically felt lump in his throat that makes it difficult to breathe. He had a history of severe asthma in his home country and he feels this medical condition was a bodily expression of his feeling of suffocation; it has not recurred since moving to London. In leaving his homeland, Martin feels clear that he was really looking for something basic about existence itself, not something as superficial as just enjoying life, since that possibility had not even occurred to him yet.

While young, Graciella's parents travelled frequently, often apart. Graciella was able to mould this situation so that she could construct a space *between* her parents that maximized her freedom. She was able to be herself in this interstitial space and thus avoided being trapped in either parent's world. Graciella began to develop this space from *nothing* into a *free space* where she could experiment with her identity without the impinging family context. She knew how to be the person each of her parents expected her to be, but adopting these identities made her feel like a foreigner in each of those contexts. She was allowed access to all of herself only in the neutral between-world she had created, but that space was ungrounded and provided no direction for her. All she knew was that she had to escape the known alternatives.

If escape in some form were not possible, participants imagined either that they would end up in conflict with their environment, or that compliance with others' expectations would result in just withering up and fading away. This highlights the depth of the feeling about the need for escape from the threat of settled life. Travel can offer magical experiences in place of the everyday settled world's lack of spontaneity, lack of joy, and loss of magic. Escape is partially a fleeing from the ordinary and everyday concerns which are experienced as petty, close-minded, and repressive. Settling in one place would require integrating extraordinary travel experiences into an ordinary daily life.

However, some conventional choices, like academic study or creative projects, which eventually facilitate further freedom, can approximate a form of palatable 'sedentary adventure'. In such cases, the motivation to engage in new avenues of self-understanding can be strong enough to help a person persevere through strong feelings of not belonging and the desire to escape. The choice to remain *put* can be a decision to invest in oneself and in the case of one participant, like one's 'last chance'. Subtle forms of 'sedentary adventure' such as actively exploring new neighbourhoods can give the breathing space needed to settle, at least temporarily, without feeling suffocated.

Both belonging (implying settling) and escape (implying travel) are complex experiences; both experiences simultaneously imply alluring and threatening possibilities. Sensitivity to suffocating forms of belonging seems to encourage these individuals to escape geographically. Even without any previous exposure to other cultures or places, some of these participants imagined their leaving as the route to self-fulfilment and freedom from incompatible surroundings. In the midst of the desperation to leave, it was difficult for most people to consciously reflect upon their actions or motives. It can be easier in hindsight to see one's process of planning and taking positive steps to rescue oneself. For some, the research interview provided the reflective space to notice the deeper meanings of leaving; in fact this form of dialogue itself seemed to provide an example of the non-intrusive relationship and respect for difference that these participants seek.

In Summary:
'Belonging' is viewed with intense ambivalence; the attraction consists in the imagined warmth and connection with others, while the repulsion is experienced as an oppressive demand to conform to the conventional and disown one's uniqueness. Ideally, belonging would incorporate acceptance of who one feels oneself to be, and the space to be that person. However, participants usually experienced a more conditional belonging, based upon 'fitting in' and this was too much of a sacrifice. Individuals experienced themselves, and were experienced by others, as different and this was one source of their feeling of not-belonging. The feeling of difference predates the experience of being rejected and it was not uncommon for participants

to say they had never felt at home in their home environment. It is very common for participants to reside in two places, have a country house, or travel frequently, in order to have a place to escape to. This seems to be one resolution of the need to belong and the need to remain apart and independent. Continually escaping can eventually limit one's investment in personal and professional development that requires committing to being in one place for a period of time. It seems that both leaving and settling incur potential threats to developing self-potential.

6.3 WHAT DO I VALUE IN LIFE?

Independence, freedom, choice, and space, are intricately interconnected, to the extent that separating them into these terms makes only a little sense. *Each demands and implicates the others.* In stories of leaving home the relationship between these concepts was often expressed by asserting that feeling independent and free permits choosing for oneself, but independence, freedom, and thus choice, require a sense of physical 'space' because for some people physical space is a requirement for psychological space.

Despite the positive associations with independence, there can also be underlying secondary motivations; that independence can signify 'retaliation' for the rejection of not belonging. The achievement of independence demonstrates that the support of others is not needed anyway. In this sense, self-reliance is partly a prophylactic against rejection and as such implies some ingredient of emotional pain. However, even in these cases, the prevailing sense is positive; independence, freedom, choice and personal space are intrinsic to life. For some participants losing their freedom can elicit deep panic, to the extreme of approximating a spiritual death.

Independence can be prioritized over family, the warmth of long-standing friendships, and the assumed comfort of a home world.

Individuals can feel proud of having the courage to escape the comfortable and the given, to carve an independent life out of nothing. The suppression implicit in staying at home is unacceptable to the individuals under consideration here. For them, such restriction generates a need to expand, or as two participants expressed, the need to 'search for a tribe' within which one might encounter similar souls and a sense of belonging without self-denial and contraction. The themes in this section reveal what participants are eager to point out; that even when family difficulties exist, they may not be the primary motive for needing to leave home, and certainly never the *sole cause*.

Rita cannot see any meaning in a life that is not self-directed, in which one takes responsibility to control what one can control, to pursue a self-generated sense of direction rather than conforming to other's agendas, fashions, or fads. It feels important to her not to be stifled by hierarchies and to resist the mainstream, not to give into the conventional and the received. She recalls a pivotal early memory of her mother telling her that she didn't need to believe the nun's religious teaching at school because she was not Catholic and this instilled the idea that authorities didn't have to be believed, one was free to discern things for oneself. At the end of life, Rita would like to look back and be able to say that she's always followed her passions with courage; this is a constant refrain supporting her life choices from early life to the present and into the future.

Giving up a settled life for solitary travel and living alone in a foreign place requires trusting one's own 'voice'. even when travel and migration has not been modelled in the original environment, certain people are tempted by a call into the foreign that issues from nowhere other than one's own self. Travelling can be an experience of being free, fending for oneself, looking after oneself, and being challenged by the differences in the world. These journeys can form the highlights of one's life; participants often referred back fondly to such adventures. At the same time travelling can teach much about the limits of one's independence, the requisite balance between solitude and companionship.

Parents can interfere with the development of personal responsibility and independence, often when it's trying to seek its first full expression in adolescence. Carl's parents tried to protect him from the transition of leaving home and taking his own personal responsibility. He knows his parents would like to maintain him in their 'safe little world', however he cannot adapt to this. It was crucial to Carl that he find his own space. His experience, corroborated by other participants, is that physical space allows mental space. It allows a person to become his or her 'own master' by securing unencumbered space and time to work through decisions without intrusions upon the self-directed nature of this process.

When Sarah moved to London, she experienced a 'heady' sense of being able to do what she wants. She doesn't have to worry about who she is all the time, or constantly battle against being overwhelmed. Freedom is highly valued by Sarah, again because it gives her the space to decide for herself, and making choices is the theme of her life. Having a choice and making it for herself is experienced as wonderful, whether it's a bad choice or good is less relevant. Predictably, Sarah does not react well to being told what to do. She needs the experience of being involved in decisions that affect her, but having had a say, she can then carry out the decision even if she disagrees with it. However, if decisions are imposed upon her, she rebels – she perceives the only possible response to external imposition is to fight for her freedom.

Even as a young child, Renata valued having her own separate space and played games with her sister using chairs and blankets to create little environments to explore. By the time she got her own bedroom in the family home it could no longer satisfy her growing need for space. Lack of space is lack of freedom, so Renata could no longer feel at peace in the family home. She could only define herself negatively, by resisting what was impinging upon her. Renata coped with the lack of space by being active in the locality and spending little time at home. Meeting an English-speaking group in her hometown offered Renata choices she'd never experienced in her protective family environment. This group offered a new world where her views were sought and valued, where she wasn't expected to acquiesce in order to belong. She now realizes that freedom is more important to her than belonging. For Renata, freedom involves being accepted as she is, with the possibility of real dialogue, whereas belonging is imposed and ritualized, with no possibility for true connection.

Specific environments can pose greater challenges, even threats, to these values of independence, freedom, and choice. For example, environments that are couple or family-oriented can feel like a burden and may be avoided by people who value their individuality and independence in the way described, even those who themselves have children and partners. An ex-pat community that tries to maintain the homogenous home culture abroad exemplifies this restrictive environment, recreating the original painful experiences of not fitting in but under the assumed cloak of being one of them. Fiona found living in an ex-pat environment unreal, frustrating, and dissatisfying because there wasn't enough encounter with the local culture and therefore inadequate exposure to difference. She had left home in order to engage in the larger cultural context, to express her desire to be socially active, but the ex-pat situation recapitulated the original limitations she had fled. When in a limiting or entrapping situation, Fiona's first response, like Sarah's, is to become active and struggle to change the parameters, expand the boundaries, regain a sense of freedom. If the limits cannot be extended, she must escape in order to live.

Issues of freedom also came up in reference to the question of whether the person ever considered returning home. Those who considered this option did so in a very specific way, so as not to recreate the original feelings of suffocation. Though many participants feel certain that they would never re-settle at 'home', some, like Martin, could imagine returning temporarily knowing he has the freedom to leave again. Although he does not miss his home culture at all, he would like to be able to visit his family more often. Likewise, Martin needs the freedom to think he might leave London at some point; that he could go to any country in the world. Having the freedom to consider that possibility allows him to feel he is making his own choices, like he is proving to himself he can make any choice he wants. For Martin, like Sarah, choice is fundamental to life, it allows him *to be*, to live life rather than just exist.

The first experience of foreign travel can be pivotal as a realization of long held dreams of independence and freedom. It can be a relief to feel able to fulfil those young ambitions to be adventurous; a whole exotic world thereby opens to exploration. Peter loved his first experience of foreign travel and appreciated his own ability to be independent and to adapt to these strange environments, languages, difficult situations and people, in a way he hadn't been able to at home. Peter's newfound confidence was essential in his choice not to pursue conventional forms of life, which he had hitherto experienced as painfully restricting. His first experience of foreign travel suggested that there might be a place where he could feel comfortable, at least a loose social nexus of mobile choices, where aspects of self can shift like a kaleidoscope, always changing what one brings and what one leaves behind. Travelling is the *living of difference*. It provides an insight into what is diverse and what is common in human life. For these individuals it offers a bigger picture, a new repertoire of choices, and an unattached reflective space.

For Francois, moving to a foreign place is partly about challenging himself to survive the unknown and unpredictable. Francois wants to constantly rise above the known into something unknown in order to 'build his character'. In order to *feel his being*, Francois needs to be challenged (reminiscent of Peter's desire to 'kick himself alive'). As soon as he's adapted to the foreign place, he needs to find something new to struggle with, a new place or project. It does not feel good enough for him to be in his 'comfort zone' (this theme is also expressed by other participants). In order to develop his capacities and continue his personal growth, he constantly requires the challenge of the new – comfort is stagnation, and stagnation is death. Francois says his individuation is about physically removing himself from the familiar in order to feel 'fresh air' again.

Looking back at his home country, Francois denigrates the lifestyle, seeing it as unaware and self-involved. There he sees a meaningless cycle of work, earning money, going home, watching TV, getting up and going to work ... This mundane life feels tranquillizing for Francois and he speculates about the dreadful unhappiness and disfigured soul he would have become if he had stayed at home. He could not accept being a stunted version of who he is now. Francois was inspired when confronted by new experiences at university, where he developed his own thinking and awareness. It 'woke him up' and now in order to stay awake Francois feels he needs to keep contacting difference, one way to do this is to keep 'flying away' to new places.

During the interview I invited participants to imagine what it would be like to stay put in a place even though it began to feel restrictive but even imagining this scenario elicited pronounced discomfort. Although imagining staying at home felt threatening and frightening, there were indications that confronting the restrictions there might also beget that elusive feeling of peace and perhaps engender new forms of freedom. Opportunities that necessitate remaining settled for a period, for example, education or a job commitment, can feel like an anchor and be both feared and appreciated at the same time. There was a suggestion that repeated geographical movement may not be the only way to express the cherished values under discussion. For example, many of the participants expressed strong values of fighting for the oppressed, and social justice. This could be perceived as an intersubjective counterpart to their own need for independence, choice, and freedom – their own experiences of these values are enhanced, even intimately connected to, others' *possibilities* of actualizing them.

For example, Rita challenges her original culture by consistently siding with marginalized traditional cultures, always wanting the Indians to win in westerns, supporting the Palestinian cause, expressing sensitivity to the plight of the oppressed. Rita has used her career to speak on behalf of the unjustly treated and dispossessed in various capacities. This sort of critique and rebellion has been an aspect of her experience from an early age but it is a mystery to her where this sensitivity comes from. Again, perhaps it's in part another expression of her sensitivity to freedom, choice, and self-determination.

In Summary:
Self-creation must prevail over belonging, security, and certainty. Anything is worth sacrificing in order to maintain the freedom to choose for oneself. Conformity to the conventional is avoided at all costs – life is meaningless unless it is self-directed. Physical space is a prerequisite for the reflective space within which self-direction manifests. Encroachment upon one's personal space elicits resistance and defence. The loss of freedom is deeply distressing, approximating the death of the 'self'. To follow the call to independence, freedom and choice, one must trust one's own voice, and have a degree of self-confidence. Moving to a foreign place and travelling internationally are archetypal situations for expressing the above needs. The challenge of unfamiliar situations offers the possibility of continuous development while the comfort of the familiar is felt as stagnation.

6.4 A WORLDWIDE PERSPECTIVE

Many individuals were aware of what could be called a 'spiritual dimension' in their experience. Some made explicit reference to a spiritual practice while others alluded to the transcendent within everyday life. Depending upon how spirituality is defined, this brief section could also be considered a preamble to the next topic, which explores 'openness to difference'. Openness to the spiritual-religious element in existence may constitute a radical appreciation of 'otherness', that which is not-me, foreign to my understanding, and yet simultaneously the very heart of me.

Homelessness was often intimately connected with the restlessness of spiritual quests and attempts to understand life through diverse beliefs and traditions. This wider perspective was also evident in less tangible ways, for example, a need to be expansive, open to the 'more' of life, following a 'calling', being attentive to the mysterious transpersonal core of life and of oneself. This theme was also commonly expressed in the negative, not being able to conform to the smallness of settled life, its mundane reduction to the everyday 'known'. Some participants concluded that conventional forms of life are spiritually vacuous, leaving something 'deeper' unaddressed and unlived.

Common sentiments in the transcripts suggest that leaving home expresses an existential facet of life – a difficult to express but clearly felt need to expand beyond the place where one is *put* to grow up. The need to leave is itself *mysterious*. To speculate: perhaps this need is an expression of inborn sensitivities, an underlying openness in one's being, a predestined nomadic path, illustrated through numerous instances of the incompatibility of a malleable self colliding with the hardness of the home environment. There is no one answer to this mystery and some participants wanted to safeguard that inscrutability. Many of them seemed willing to live with a curious '*I don't know*' regarding why they had to leave rather than pin it down with a conclusive explanation. Nina believes that life is governed by a 'calling' and this can be trusted as a guide to one's choices. It's an intuitive sense that seems to connect the self and the larger world, an invisible web within which individual lives are choreographed. This raises a question of how much the individual needs to make conscious decisions (apart from the constant choice to heed and trust this calling) and to what extent events will unfold along lines that are determined by transcendent interconnections beyond our grasp. Nina feels that travelling out in the wider world exposes a person to the deeper mysteries of life in a way that remaining settled does not.

Graciella and Anna were explicit about the spiritual aspect of their migrations. For Anna, even at a young age, she chose to dedicate herself to living in foreign cultures renowned for their spirituality and to shun the conventional religious beliefs of her own culture. These spiritual yearnings lead her on a quest that distanced her further from others at home. She was isolated and misunderstood and the pain of this fortified her predisposition to leave. But what exposed her to a dimension of life that others around her seemed oblivious to? Why should *she* be different?

This spiritual quest entails a number of sacrifices. For Anna it involved abandoning her family and her conventional education in exchange for enduring years of isolation and travel. However, she has no regrets about her decision, it was what she 'had' to do. Graciella also understands her leaving home as part of a larger spiritual predestination linked with her beliefs. She believes that she was *born to leave* in order to work through issues of 'home'. Graciella needed to gain courage from her home circumstances before she was ready to journey out into the world. There was a match between what Graciella needed from her origins and what her family needed from her. She needed to be like a butterfly for them, so there was never any contemplation of not leaving; it had to be this way for life to unfold as it should.

As an adolescent, Ben sought psychic and spiritual beliefs very much on the margins of his society. These rare sources of spiritual difference bolstered him to cope with the uniformity of his young life. They expressed his innate compulsion for more conscious living. This attraction to the psychic sphere addressed an aspect of Ben that was impoverished in his contact with peers, family, and general cultural values. This attraction to mystery is similar to Ben's perpetual need to experience the unfamiliar through travel and living in foreign places. The seduction of a place, or a belief, can be temporary, soon instigating another round of exploration, and in the interview Ben mentions that he has yet to explore the East, where he anticipates deeper esoteric difference may await him.

Peter was always attracted to what he did not understand; an affinity to everything mysterious and to what must remain unknown. This included his experience of himself as emotionally incoherent and thus a mystery. For example, Peter continues to try to understand his sense of alienation in his original home place. He feels strangely comforted by any experience of mystery since it matches the mystery he finds when he explores himself. This comfort arises from the affirmation that mystery is an acceptable part of the universe and therefore he is acceptable. Since Peter experiences himself as an enigma, being in a mystifying foreign place creates a match between the external world he experiences and his own being. This 'match' is like a kind of equivalency that makes him feel at home. For Peter, and I would argue perhaps for all of us, *feeling at home is the experience of this interaction of the inner and outer matching in idiosyncratic ways*[12]. 'Matching', of course, does not imply sameness; what it implies may be different for each person, different at different times, and not predictable beforehand. For Peter, the nearest experience of home is his connection with this intimate communion of mysteries. He belongs within the whole human and inhuman world and the impermanence of everything.

---

12. This will be discussed in a later chapter as a major new understanding - home as interaction, rather than *home as place* or home as 'inner peace'.

These experiences embody the spiritual dimension of feeling 'at home' in an unfathomable world, a kind of home within homelessness.

Returning home can also have a 'spiritual' dimension. Fiona feels that her leaving home was connected to the experience of diaspora that runs through her home culture. Part of Fiona's spiritual journey is to find her individual place in that historical narrative. Her aesthetic appreciation for the landscape of her homeland remains stronger than her connection to any other physical geography in the world. In that ancestral place Fiona feels whole, like finding the piece to a puzzle. The experience of returning 'home' has opened Fiona to speculations about cross-generational healing, returning to address psychological difficulties not only of ones' own, but also of parents and more distant ancestors. Her mission in this regard has an intuitive feel to it, as though the wanderer seeks to heal emotional memories of *attachment to place* that are somehow transmitted through generations.

In Summary:
Leaving home can be the expression of a spiritual quest that cannot be undertaken within the confines of the home environs. Exploring the world can be guided by an 'inner calling' that feels like an intuitive connection to a transpersonal dimension. Some participants explain their migrations as components of the teachings of spiritual traditions and practices which are not native to their home cultures and which result in their further marginalization. Travel is a valued mode of 'conscious living', keeping a person aware of surroundings and preventing a slip into habitual and less mindful ways of living. Seeking out contact with unfamiliar and mysterious cultures offers an external experience of the mystery one finds within one's own being and the deeper mysteries of the world. This matching between person and world can generate a temporary feeling of belonging in the universe. This suggests a new definition of 'home' as interaction. The return home, after years abroad, can signify spiritual reconnection and psychological healing of self, family, and even the healing of cultural history, for example the trauma of forced mass migration.

6.5 LOVE OF DIFFERENCE AND FOREIGNNESS

Existential migration is typified by a pronounced affinity for difference, a curiosity for and attraction to the foreign and unfamiliar, coupled with disdain for ways of living that orbit around the familiar and known. This incessant regard for the foreign and unfamiliar distinguishes the existential migrant from their social and family environments, which are built upon commonality. *This 'love of difference' is a difference that makes a difference.* It can elicit rejecting attitudes from 'homogenous' cultures; *an attraction to difference sets one apart as different*, and this reinforces the need to leave, for all the reasons described in earlier chapters.

There is a pay-off as well as a price to pay for being different. Along with the painful discomfort and confusion of not-belonging, almost from birth it would seem in some cases, there is also a notion that being different connotes being special and excuses one from mundane and meaningless conventions. But even in existential migration there exists a tacit attraction to similarity in the tendency to seek out people and places that likewise celebrate 'difference', within which the common attribute of not-belonging is the form of belonging.

Ben provides an eloquent and representative description of many of the nuances encompassed within the 'lure of difference'. Ben grew up in a very homogenous town, where he lived in the same house until he left home. Within this sea of similarity, Ben remembers valuing any source of difference, and was excited on the rare occasions that a student from a different culture or race moved to town. Ben even felt that other places within his homeland were more interesting than his own locality. He could not understand why *anyone* would *choose* to live where he did. It was always disappointing to return home.

Ben needed to get away from this familiar world, which dictated what his identity should be. He longed for an environment within which he could re-invent himself. The future he anticipated at home was laid out before him as totally predictable and boring. Ben felt a deep liberation when he finally moved across country and left behind everyone who knew him, and their constraining preconceptions. He began to feel free to realize the difference within him, transforming his appearance and beliefs, and seeking new experiences in celebration of his liberation from the home environment.

At the age of 19 Ben met a group of foreign students and this opened his eyes to the possibilities of foreign travel. He was tremendously excited by the challenge these students offered to the concepts and assumptions of his own society. This exposure to disparate cultures galvanized Ben's quest for adventure, peaking in his departure for Europe. Though he had not spent his youth consciously planning an escape from his homeland, he also never once imagined he would stay there. Meeting these students activated Ben's nascent life trajectory and off he flew, as he implicitly assumed he always would.

Ben migrated to France, which was the pinnacle of his early adult experience, partly because it challenged the puritanical values of his original home. He states that France was a more appropriate 'match' for his values than his own culture, so paradoxically the foreign country, by being different from his home culture, was actually more similar to 'Ben' as the person he felt himself to be. Herein lies the understated motif of the need for *similar values within the attraction to difference* – the valued sameness that is needed is the shared value of *accepting difference* in contrast to sameness as conformity. This incorporation of 'sameness' within an attraction to difference is shared by a number of participants and echoes many existential migrants' desires for the familiar in the strange and the strange in the familiar. This will be explored more in part two of the book.

Ben wonders if he had grown up in France would he be attracted to America instead, the suggestion being that his sensitivity to difference is in part a construction in opposition to the prevailing culture, no matter which culture. He admits that he likes being different, to stand out and get attention in a positive way, so the attraction to difference can be thought of as partially an incorporation of the exotic in order to appear special. For example, Ben mentions returning home with his foreign partner and his partner receiving more attention because she stands out as comparatively more different than Ben and Ben finds that usurpation from his special status to be uncomfortable.

Continental Europe is ideal for Ben since it offers the close proximity of a cluster of differences, in terms of a menagerie of values, lifestyles, and especially languages. We will see that linguistic difference has also been a significant motivator for other participants. Ben loves the accessibility of moving from one language world into another just by hopping on a train. Ben finds this diversity very exciting but he finds his own excitement about this to be quite mysterious. He is able to recount many examples of experiences of crossing borders into a new language but the underlying *meaning* of his excitement is elusive. Ben can only say that he experiences something magical about the proximity of these cultural transitions. He speculates that an aspect of the attraction to this multi-linguistic environment is its stark contrast with his more 'monochromatic' home culture where acceptable minor differences are held within an overall cultural sameness; a form of sameness that Ben found suffocating.

Ben now lives in London, where his social life is populated by a group of international friends. And again, underlying these obvious national differences are fundamental shared values of tolerance and social liberalism. Though this similar perspective on the world is a necessary aspect of belonging to this group, each person's original culture is inconsequential, except that there must be cultural diversity. It is plausible that creating this sense of belonging *within* diversity achieves the sought-after *acceptance of difference*.

This highlights the fact that difference, and being different, is preferred when it signifies acceptance but not when it elicits rejection. So it is not surprising that Ben is exhausted by repeatedly having to overcome negative assumptions about himself solely because of his birthplace. In his international social set, Ben's homeland implies negative values of intolerance and provincial attitudes, forcing Ben into a position of having to *prove* a *basic similarity* in outlook in order for his difference to be accepted. Ben must demonstrate his allegiance to diversity by distancing himself from his home culture, in essence saying, my values are your values – I'm not one of *them*, thus 'betraying' the culture of origin, which had originally betrayed him.

Carl made strong meaningful bonds with friends outside the home. Some of these friends did not fit with his family mores, so his parents banned them from visiting the family home. For Carl this elicited a conflict between his valued openness to diversity and his parent's demand for homogeneity, creating a difficult choice for him between loved parents and loved friends. In these divided loyalties, Carl acknowledges that the security offered by his idyllic family life was clashing with his growing identification with marginality and the world outside the exclusivity of his home. For some people the walls around the home are where the world ends - for others it's where the world begins. Carl was fascinated by views that diverged from those expressed in his safe family enclave but his parents reacted by trying to silence his emerging voice and this was very painful for Carl. This censorship accentuated his marginality within the home, increasing his identification with others who are different. Carl hypothesizes that people who are 'different' have somehow been 'opened up' by life's betrayals, opened by experiencing a context in which they don't belong, and consequently living with the threat of things falling apart. This openness to life manifests as a fundamental questioning about life, queries about meaning and purpose - why are we here, what should we do, how should we live? This encounter with 'openness' is not easily understood and Carl suggests that it could equally be conceptualized as a kind of impaired ability to just accept the taken for granted view of things.

In her hometown, Rita was disgusted by 'small-minded racist attitudes' and partly as a challenge to these attitudes she had a Black boyfriend while still living at home. Rita's academic and career choices certainly reflect her personal sensitivities to difference. She seeks out new situations, new horizons and projects, through her career as an international development worker. This accords her frequent opportunities to travel and exposure to cosmopolitan worlds diametrically opposite to her upbringing. She now supports many marginalized and vulnerable people in other parts of the world. It is a mystery to Rita where this proclivity to otherness and social justice comes from. She continues to choose to live in places that are culturally very mixed and vibrant, worlds within worlds. Rita feels more 'at home' in diverse cosmopolitan environments offering more fluid possibilities for identity, less restriction or pressure to conform to one monolith and this seems consistent with a need for space, freedom, and independence.

Of course there is significant individual uniqueness about how these sensitivities are expressed; existential migration is not one concrete thing, not a diagnosis. Existential migration itself is very diverse. For example, Kathy's life demonstrates a unique kind of sensitivity to difference and foreignness. As a young girl, Kathy had positive experiences of travelling across country with her swimming club. Her experience of travel gave her the opportunity to bond with like-minded people, a combination of being with similarity while encountering difference, which is a dynamic that continues now in migrations with her husband (together they share a very similar outlook on the world while travelling globally). As with other participants, Kathy can't explain the meaning of her love of travel, except that travel constitutes a form of escape for her. Again this is escape from the ordinary everydayness of life. Travel constitutes a break from the stresses and boredom of routine daily living. She is constantly pulled towards unfamiliar cultures, places, religions, people, but she does not understand the basis of this attraction. Also, like Ben, Kathy finds most of her friendships are with others like herself, internationalists and mixed-culture couples.

Moving to a new culture and learning a new language offers Kathy the type of challenge she needs, but once accomplished the everyday quotidian routines intrude again and this is experienced as soul-destroying. Kathy creates higher and higher goals to see where her limits are. She is competitive and she acknowledges that this is an expression of the cultural values of her home country. It is worth noting that in all the material that has arisen from these interviews, there is great diversity, not only due to biographical details and individual idiosyncrasy, but also from the inevitable influence of the original, and usually rejected, culture. We all start from somewhere[13] and leaving home does not eradicate its influence.

For many of the participants, frustration eventually resurfaces in response to the less desirable aspects of the new culture. It is disappointing when many of the negative cultural attributes one was circumventing through emigration return one by one to haunt the person in the new place. Kathy has felt this in every place she has lived, gradually experiencing the place as too homogenous, middle-class, conformist, small-minded, or lacking in spontaneity, expression, and dynamic energy. Kathy recognizes that the way she and her husband live in a place is 'aloof', maintaining maximum freedom from the local culture, non-attachment and anonymity, but thereby also foregoing the support of the local culture and any potential sense of belonging. In the end perhaps for some of us no *one* place is 'good enough' and constant mobility is the best alternative.

---

13. A discussion of the impact of our starting place is taken up in Part Two.

Curiosity has always been fundamental to Kathy's self-experience though again she does not understand the core of this. Curiosity is expressed through the variety of her travels, her studies, her ability to speak different languages, and her range of different careers. Kathy expressed a desire to be less curious so that she could be satisfied and settle down. She describes herself as a 'global nomad', a contemporary term in the new service industry of 'international relocation consulting'. There may be a discrepancy between *existential migration* and being a *global nomad*. For example, existential migration signifies a deeply felt searching or yearning that expresses and addresses something in existence itself. The global nomad appears less purposive in his or her movement, more motivated by superficial curiosity and conventional values, tinged with the need to escape *from* but without the meaningful and self-reflective motivation evident in existential migration.

As an immigrant to Europe, Valerie's mother attempted to deny her own foreignness by adopting the host European culture when Valerie was a child. This seems to have been a significant process for Valerie to witness. Valerie has not attempted to 'homogenize' herself into sameness as her mother attempted to do, but consequentially she feels like a broken jigsaw, a mixture of places and cultures, an odd person of bits and pieces from everywhere and thus nowhere. Her mother downplayed her own cultural origin to the extent that her children did not even recognize her cultural difference or even her different ethnicity. Such an obvious denial of difference may give the message that belonging requires homogeneity, and difference will be rejected.

Valerie feels inferior and frustrated when she doesn't understand the shared subtle cues of a homogenous group. This experience can be so alienating that, like Camilla, Valerie can begin to feel she doesn't even belong on the planet. Languages continue to change and evolve. Not feeling up-to-date and fluent in any one language can affect one's sense of belonging anywhere, but making it easier to live in places where there are many non-native speakers so that one at least 'belongs' in this shared 'incompetence'. Valerie notices that her feeling of foreignness is comparative – feeling less foreign around someone who is more foreign than her, and feeling more foreign around someone who is totally native, this applies even in the place she grew up. Sometimes 'foreigner' can be a label applied from the inside, even at home.

Participants who are not native English speakers described learning the English language as an exciting entry point into a different world. For example, Inez found it very challenging when she was confronted with not being able to understand an English-speaking group visiting her country. Their use of English enchanted Inez, as it seemed to offer a more empowered form of expression and greater self-confidence than her native tongue. Inez felt that English offered the possibility of saying things she valued which she couldn't express in her own language. The challenge to communicate was exciting, confronting Inez with experiences of a new and much more attractive world. She was so inspired to explore the world of English that she decided to leave her home, family, and fiancé, to study in the UK. In this case, language is the medium of the attraction to otherness. Inez experienced her own language as subdued, reflecting her place in her home and social environment. To her, English was the language of power and equality, and learning this new language symbolized freedom from her own world and its values. It was the language of the world and thus a doorway into larger possibilities. In meeting this English-speaking group, life for Inez suddenly became divided between the excitement of foreignness and conforming to the expectations of her native society. For the first time she was able to consider a choice between two forms of life. As Inez compared the two worlds, she found that the foreign group offered a sense of 'true' belonging, excitement and vitality, and an experience of the magic of *real* communication, which she had never had in her home environment. Her home world felt stifling, reserved, and conservative, a straightforward life of acquiescing to traditional expectations.

Marta was also attracted to the UK because she wanted to live in an English-speaking country. The foreign language was a very important part of her desire to stay, though she's not sure why. She liked the difference of English, its cleanly spoken pronunciation compared to the difficult sounds of her own language. It seems easier, more fluent, controlled and appropriate, whereas her native language is a struggle and it's hard for Marta to even speak it now. Speaking English fluently enabled Marta to fit in *and* permitted her to leave behind aspects of her self that were wedded to her native language. Recently Marta has come to resent this adaptation to Englishness and the subsequent loss of her native 'self'. She no longer wants to adapt to the indigenous English society surrounding her. She gets emotional about the loss of her own language and her devaluing of it. After some years in England, she feels that she now has some insight into what lies behind the well-spoken English and she purposely tries to disrupt this pretence and instead wants to stand out as different. Language can be a potent symbol for the appropriations and losses implicit in choosing to become a foreigner. Marta's feelings about English and her native language are shifting as she ages and she now begins to appreciate the full cost of leaving her home culture.

Martin still seeks an explanation for his difference, as if there really could be a satisfying answer. It is not surprising that one of Martin's main questions remains 'is difference OK?' The message from his environment was that difference is unacceptable and he internalized this message and labelled himself as 'weird'. For Martin, foreigners were different in a positive sense since they represented a world rich in choices. He had a very positive image of that world despite its harsh competitiveness. In contrast, Martin grew up to believe that he deserved to be punished for his own difference.

Graciella expresses a common sentiment when she explains that visits home leave her feeling both reconnected and also disconnected and foreign. For example, the relations between men and women have a specific character in her country. Graciella has always had relationships with men from other cultures and they have always communicated together in English, their shared third language. Partly due to her dissatisfaction with this, she now considers that having a relationship with a man from her own country might have positive aspects. For example, she wouldn't have to explain or educate him about cultural nuances; they could take for granted some common cultural understanding, which would be a relief. Graciella also fantasizes about the romance of being in a relationship expressed in her own first language, where she could hear and say the things she heard her parents say to each other when she was young. She wonders if she would still have to hide herself and if she would still feel misunderstood in such a relationship. She realizes that over the years she has been domesticated by other cultures and is no longer very typical of the temperament of her home country. It is possible that the shared commonality she could have in a relationship with a fellow countryman is forever gone due to her increasing elaboration as a complex migratory self. Graciella eventually concludes that it's not the place one comes from, nor any easily defined external characteristics that are *most* important. It's a vibrating and resonating energy between people that she longs for, and difference is not a barrier as long as it's difference within this deeper energetic connection. Graciella feels she can recognize this 'energy' in people and that these people form a kind of international *tribe*. She feels most isolated and lonely when she doesn't have others of her 'tribe' around her. This is a theme that emerges repeatedly throughout the interviews; there exists a loose 'grouping' that does not identify itself as a group, yet the members of this 'group' can *recognize each other*. Individuals engaged in what I term 'existential migration' have a pronounced tendency to associate with others who have made similar choices, who 'vibrate with a similar energy'. Though Graciella considers the possibility that the similarity amongst one's countrymen could enhance the depth of an intimate relationship, she ends up deciding, along with other participants, that there is a more essential and intangible quality of 'tribeness' that is more significant than cultural similarity when choosing partners and friends.

People who are not 'existential migrants' usually assume everyone has a deep innate affinity to cultural similarity and familiarity. But this is the polar opposite of the dynamic attraction to difference expressed by existential migrants. For the majority of the settled population, the similarity that is felt with others in one's native land offers a deep and crucial undercurrent that feels connecting. This connection with the similar offers belonging based upon similarity rather than the complex belonging expressed above, which includes an attraction to the foreign, the unfamiliar, and the diverse.

In Summary:
Existential migrants display a marked preference for the unfamiliar, often finding their values better reflected in foreign cultures or other languages rather than in their own home cultures or families. Often these voluntary migrants coalesce together in informal international groups with pronounced cultural diversity but within underlying similarities in terms of accepting difference and valuing otherness. Being perceived as different is valued when it confers a special status but difference more often results in painful rejection. Continually encountering unfamiliar cultures is a way of remaining 'conscious', 'awake', and not falling into habitual modes of life that feel boring and predictable. Linguistic differences can be enticing, promising a gateway to new cultures and a whole world of new experience. There is the haunting unanswered question of why these specific individuals exhibit these values; why, often in the midst of a milieu that values similarity, should these people deeply value the opposite?

6.6 ORIGINS - EARLY FAMILY AND HOME CIRCUMSTANCES

It is too simplistic to leap from the circumstances of family life to causal explanations about why a person chooses to leaves home. We have seen that the process of 'existential migration' encompasses something complex and mysterious, interwoven with complicated biographical circumstances, and facilitated by the potential for travel.

Many of the participants who mention the significance of their childhood experiences explicitly caution us not to narrow down the whole matrix of this complex phenomenon down to an archaeology of primary bonds and 'individual *defect*'. If certain early experiences *caused* the choice to leave one's home country, we should see a discernable pattern, but no such simplistic pattern emerges. Many family members, including siblings of these participants, have similar early experiences but never consider leaving their home culture. In fact most of the participants continually strive for understanding from these close relations who cannot comprehend their choice to leave.

While early relationships are undoubtedly important, I would contend that *our childhood relationships are as much expressions of our orientations toward the world as they are formative of them.* All our attempts to understand even a moment of human life remain at best *metaphors* for what inevitably remains more complex and elusive than any theory. So as not to be misled by facile assumptions of cause and effect, we will endeavour to remain *close to what the participants themselves* say about the significance of their family relationships.

Problems in the parents' relationship can hasten a pre-existing inclination to leave home. Eva was relieved when her parents finally divorced, even though this stigmatized the family within their neighbourhood, contributing further to the social alienation she felt. The resulting situation necessitated that Eva grow up quickly, exaggerating her feelings of independence and freedom without a counterbalancing sense of connection to others. Eva is certain that moving away was not her attempt to track down and replace the missing stability in her own home life, but she does admit that she would have felt more grounded if she had secure familial relationships that she could trust. Feelings about her national culture are closely connected with the quality of Eva's relationships with her family – but over the years these family relations are gradually transforming, facilitating her feeling more at home in her own culture again.

The reactions of parents, brothers and sisters, and other family members can make it either easier or more difficult to leave home. Complex feelings arise from knowing that it is necessary to leave home while also being aware that the home environment will not easily let go. In order to avoid painful conflict, surreptitious modes of leaving, posing as unplanned and accidental, transpire. For example, extending travelling plans or commencing a relationship with someone who lives in another locale can quietly facilitate the necessary leaving without upsetting family with the whole truth all at once. This discloses the various layers of truth and concealment embedded within the intricacy of our stories of leaving home. Most participants began their interview by presenting a prima facie straightforward account of leaving home, for example to attend university or as the prolongation of a trip abroad, only to eventually reveal a much deeper and more mysterious rationale for their leaving.

Patricia had to leave in a way that didn't disrupt her valued relationship with her father and also mollified extended family members. There can be a delicate negotiation by the voluntary migrant to keep intact the myth that the new place could never be home and that one's original home is always better. Patricia's positive experience of living in London had to be hidden from the family left behind. Desperate attempts to try to explain the need to leave seldom end satisfactorily. Patricia found that her strong relationship to her father helped her keep alive certain aspects of her relationship to the home country. When her father died, part of that relationship to the home country also died, and his death obviously reinvigorated reflection on her relations to 'home'. Patricia was not the only participant who experienced the relationship to the 'home' culture as mediated through relationship to one or both parents, and vice versa, relationships to parents being equally impacted by one's feelings about the home culture. This dynamic suggests that connections to family and to nation could both express an even deeper dynamic, the orientation of the individual toward existence itself.

It requires considerable courage to be the first in the family to travel abroad or migrate if no one else has previously modelled these choices. Christine needed physical distance from her family relationships in order to gain emotional space and a new perspective on life. For example, Christine felt a huge relief when she was able to escape from the gravitational pull of her mother's orbit and settle in a geographic location far enough away to be free of her mother's influence, but close enough to visit home. Christine was the first in her family to move away and making the choice to leave felt like breaking a taboo. Christine, more than anyone else, needed emancipation from the stifling oppression at home. Why, even after she left, did she remain the only child in her family to take this route to self-development? Her siblings stayed behind, coping in their own way, unable to contemplate for themselves the step that their sister had made.

A relationship with a parent can be very difficult and painful without it being the primary reason for leaving home. In Peter's relationship with his father, the child-parent roles were reversed. This was very confusing for Peter as a child, to feel in competition with his father for his mother's attention, to feel intellectually superior to his father and yet also fearful because he sensed this was an inversion of what he should naturally expect as a child. It was clear to Peter that his father was not comfortable with his fatherly role and this had a huge emotional impact on Peter. In turn he felt uncomfortable in his father's care and did not know how to cope with his father's inability to cope with him. It is debatable how much a conflicted parental relationship contributes to the desire to escape the home environment. Peter feels that his father does not see him for the person he really is and Peter notices that he also changes to become someone slightly different around his father. There is little authentic meeting, father to son, or son to father.

Peter also feels largely alienated from the experiences of others in his extended family; they do not understand him or even want to, leaving him to assume the label of 'world traveller' in order to be comprehended, however artificial and over-simplifying this label is for him. It is true to say that this lack of understanding is reciprocal in that Peter also finds this family-centred cozy home atmosphere frustrating, unfulfilling, and boring. In general, Peter feels let down by his parents' lack of awareness of his need for practical support, their lack of understanding of his experiences, their apparent lack of interest in his projects and his life. It's as if they are frightened to really *know* their own son, and that keeps the interaction superficial and further alienates Peter. Opening up to knowing him as he actually is, would entail his parents opening up to his difference. It seems that his parents are unable to parent Peter as *their* child, to know how to nurture him or balance his inordinate sense of independence with their attempts to care, and this has continues to be emotionally painful for Peter.

Peter always knew he must leave, but he does not understand why this was inevitable for him; it feels beyond any motive or any rationale he could construct. He grew up with this internal sense of 'far-sickness', which served to further dislocate him from home. Peter makes it clear that his need to leave was not a reaction to lapsed parenting, nonetheless, 'leaving' did allow him to punish his parents for what they did not provide, and to demonstrate that he is indeed able to live without them. But Peter had to plan an escape that would meet his needs; specifically, he had to seek a land whose foreignness would feel nourishing. The foreign place must be alien enough to free him from any expectation that he *should* be able to adapt, in effect making it more likely that he could. Paradoxically, Peter actually felt he could cope in very alien places yet couldn't manage the familiarity of his own home world. It can feel like a profound release to be in a foreign place where the expectation is that one *should have* difficulties coping, whereas at home not coping constitutes '*mal*adaptation'. Since leaving home, Peter has been freed from the responsibility that plagued him as a child. He can now enjoy the dreamed-for foreign world he had fantasized about, and consoled himself with, when young.

As a three-year-old Kathy moved in with her mother and new stepfather's family. In this new family constellation, Kathy felt on the outside looking in. In response, Kathy created places where she could belong, in close friendships, with friends' families, in the social milieu surrounding sports; she created an alternative to having a settled unitary home. At times Kathy now wishes she could relax more and feel more settled in one place but doesn't think she could ever be that way. In such an account it is tempting to perceive a causal link between Kathy's early experience and later lifestyle. But it is more complicated than simple cause and effect. Even in Kathy's case her particular response to her situation was unique, her siblings did not do what she did. There are convincing clues from various interviews that pre-existing sensitivities contribute to one's way of experiencing difficult family situations. Perhaps early environment lifts out some given sensitivities while inhibiting other processes, influencing our subsequent readiness to pursue other lands. It is likely that reducing this whole process to personality trait or inhospitable family dynamics is far too simplistic. It is likely that the *interaction* between person and environment is relevant in unfolding biography. The on-going dynamics already, at an early stage, consist of our responses and responses to responses, so that individual sensitivities and environmental circumstances are already intertwined and continuously elaborated (not to mention cultural, social, and historical influences).

In contrast to Kathy (and partially illustrating the ideas outlined above), Inez had a central role in her traditional family – a secure home life bound by a loving mother and father. However, Inez felt herself in the role of 'the strong one' among the children, taking responsibility to attend to the wellness of others rather than looking after her own needs. As the eldest, Inez looked after her sisters, becoming invisible in the process (not unlike Kathy, but in a very different way). Although she has a good relationship with her family now, Inez still feels she's not quite a real person to them. Inez expressed very strong emotions during the interview when she realized that by leaving home she was in fact *choosing to exist*. She was heeding a call to save her self from a life of ghostly servitude to others' expectations. *Choosing* her own existence is crucial for Inez and worth the conflict it caused with her loved ones. Subsequently, now from her own painful experiences as a parent, Inez appreciates how difficult it was for her parents to see her go but she is grateful for the life she's had as a result.

Rita cannot fathom her mother's rejection of her unorthodox and rebellious lifestyle. After all, her mother had a very unconventional upbringing, but unlike Rita her mother's response was to value the conventional, which she continually tries to impose upon her daughter. This issue of whether to conform remains an issue in Rita's relationship to her mother. It influences Rita's belief that if an adult child ever returns to the parental home, their world will shrink back to the childhood one, casting off all the accumulated experiences of adulthood. Her nightmare scenario is to be forced to return home for some reason and to be looked after by her parents. In that situation, Rita's cosmopolitan worldly life would be swamped by her mother's recital of the little occurrences of her own conventional life in the village. Rita recognizes there are unresolved communication issues in her family, but seems to hold little hope of them shifting. Thus, the need to maintain distance from her family (conventional homogeneity) combined with the attractions of the wider world (stimulating diversity) keeps Rita away.

Carl finds it interesting to wonder why he's always had a longing to go out into the world and what impact his early family dynamics had on his later choices in this regard. Carl explains that when young, he bonded strongly with his mother. He feels it was not beneficial for him to know so much about his mother's internal life at such a young age. This feeling amplified his desire to free himself by leaving. Unlike the rest of his family, Carl has also always had very strong and intimate relationships with friends outside the family confines. Early in his life he developed the concept that family is something constructed and chosen, not defined just by blood lineage or relatives. He was sustained by his chosen friendships when his family position became unstable but this experience of shifting his security from family to a new network of intimate friendships was frightening.

Fiona feels that her attraction to otherness stems from her childhood experiences of resettling in an unknown place, surrounded by strangers, every five years or so. In her adult life, she notices that she is inclined to relocate after a few years in a place, suggesting that she now chooses a transience that was originally forced upon her. When she foresees the impulse to leave it comes as a passion. This process of transience has a limiting side; Fiona feels she repeatedly puts herself back to square one, preventing strong roots from developing anywhere, a pattern that she relates to her early history of recurring temporary attachments though her siblings experienced this also and did not follow in her footsteps.

Graciella's family is disparate and large, and this disparity leads to Graciella wanting a more integrated life. She sees her spiritual interests as an attempt to find her 'whole self' in contrast to her fragmented experience of family life. Graciella feels her reasons for leaving are complicated and may be partly related to her family. She felt she needed to grow, to experience broader perspectives, and this felt positive. But she feels she was also making a statement to her parents. When she left, she expected she would be away for a few years before returning, and this celebrated *homecoming* featured as an important aspect of her statement to her parents. She considers that perhaps her need to make this statement to them has defined her life. Though the content of the message is not clear, her leaving is like the writing on the wall, it demonstrates something elusive and profound to her family. Graciella also feels she inherited two important personal characteristics from her family experiences; courage and melancholia, and these are powerfully illustrated in her memories of witnessing her elderly grandmother sit by the front door with her bags packed waiting for someone to take her 'home'.

Like most of the participants, Sarah makes it explicitly clear that she did not relocate half way around the world just to get away from her family; however, it was a significant benefit to her to feel freed from their orbit of influence so she could discover herself. Sarah's experience of adolescence was difficult. She was unable to develop any *positive* space of her own; unable to develop her own interests and desires, and there was a sense of annihilation in this. Though she could have found a place in her homeland to develop her potential, she feels that she has finally become herself because she has chosen to live on the other side of the world. Sarah and her partner recognize that their relationship is built upon their very different early family experiences and the conflation of their different cultures give birth to novel combinations of similarity and difference within their relational dynamics. For Sarah a crucial difference between being with her partner or being with her family is that her partner does not insist on influencing her life decisions, and she values having so much freedom within relationship. Sarah thinks it's significant that she's chosen a partner who is the opposite extreme to her parents.

Marta's mother encouraged her desire to come to England, but she did not foresee the side effect that it also freed Marta to find herself. Now, at this point in her life, Marta would like to clarify something about her relationship with her mother but her feeling is that her mother is avoiding this; in fact she senses that her mother is afraid of really knowing who her daughter is. Marta is very emotional during the interview when she discusses the link between her leaving and her relationship to her mother. She understands that her mother had to cut off her feelings for her as a way of coping with her continued absence from home. Marta's perception of her mother is altering significantly now - she sees her mother as elderly and it pains her to acknowledge how absent she has been over the years. Marta cautions her own young daughter about the costs of leaving home, though her daughter already expresses a fondness for Marta's home country, which is both moving and frightening for Marta.

It is apparent how easily we could reduce accounts of leaving home to only the effect of early family circumstances. If we start by assuming it's all about family we will find it's all about family. However, replacing this section back into the whole constellation of emerging themes, we see a more complicated scenario, not readily reduced to any one cluster of explanations. The intricate elaborations that develop out of early child-environment interactions are evident in every human life, not just these lives. The importance of family (as well as peer) relationships is evident, but it also raises questions – 'Why, of all the siblings, did *this* person leave?' Looking back at previous themes a picture seems to emerge. *Something* about these individuals sets them apart and perhaps influences their strong empathetic or conflicting interactions with caregivers. Consistent attributes seem to include: an abiding sensitivity to relationships, the need for freedom and space to direct their life choices, an affinity to life's mystery and difference, the call of the 'self' to express its potential. All of this in interaction with homogeneous cultures and/or suffocating or absent parenting seems to increase the likelihood of leaving home and of not feeling 'at home' in the first place.

In Summary:
Early relationships: familial, parental, and peer, are frequently implicated in the act of leaving home or at least the timing of the departure. It is unclear to what extent difficulties in these relations are expressions of a primordial

desire to leave rather than contributing to the desire to leave. Perhaps it is both. Participants acknowledged that early parental relationships often had an impact on their plans to leave but frequently cautioned that their feelings about home and travel cannot be reduced to these early dynamics. Difficult family circumstances seemed to coalesce around pre-existing sensitivities in those who left, differentiating them from siblings who stayed. Relations with the home culture and parental relationships can become intermingled, so that an attitude of needing space from one is generalized to needing space from the other. Both can feel intrusive and conforming for people who have strong values of independence and self-direction. A feeling of not-belonging in the home environment can reinforce interests in the outside larger world, making departure into the wide world feel more urgent.

6.7 MAIN ISSUES OF HOME AND HOMECOMING

The possibility of returning home has always been an issue for me, always the horizon against which I experience my being away. Nearing the end of this research project I decided to return home and accept a faculty position at the university where I'd been an undergraduate student twenty years earlier. In retrospect I felt I needed to return, to *settle* something that would have otherwise haunted me. I lasted eighteen months. The issue had been addressed, at least as much as it ever could be. I had to return but I didn't have to stay. I left my homeland yet again, for the adventures of a more exciting world than home could ever offer me. This time the migration was less hopeful, less infused with the expectation that I would find a home and more accepting of the homelessness I live with, whether I'm in Canada or England, or some yet undiscovered vista.

The question of returning home is as vexing for voluntary migrants as it is for refugees, or migrant workers. Obsession with the question of return and the magnetism of the original place lurks near the surface for each of the individuals interviewed – return either as a desired future possibility, a work in progress, an unlikely option, or an unequivocal threat.

Interesting to note that many of these participants report never really feeling 'at home' and yet they have a fairly clear notion of what would constitute the feeling of being-at-home, should it materialize. Perhaps this indicates that irrespective of biographical experience, there is an 'existential inheritance' of a *felt sense* of home, a situation that is continually implied regardless of whether we've ever actually experienced it. Perhaps it is a mirror reflection from the undercarriage of human being itself? Are some of us doomed to the disappointment of searching for what can never be realized? At the very least, responses to the issue of home and return seem to express something essential about humanity in general.

Nina describes home as a fusion of 'physical place' and 'social space'. To feel 'at home' is to feel safe (relaxed and calm), to have free expression, to form a secure base from which one can connect to the rest of the world and explore it. Nina did not have this kind of home where she grew up. Christine imagines home as a place where it is possible to really relax and recuperate from the constant effort of living. For her, the feeling of wanting to return home for a visit is partially motivated by a need to be looked after, to be nourished by all the little niceties and routines of settled life. She believes that the importance of this reconnection might reduce if she felt more nurtured out in the foreign world where she actually lives. Leaving home has been difficult and lonely but it has also liberated Christine from the disappointment of an unsatisfying original experience of home.

Renata also describes home as a place where one is confident. She feels some sense of being at home in London since she can now navigate the city with some familiarity and she knows how to look after herself here. Familiarity, in this sense, is something about the atmosphere of a place, not something as concrete as knowing street names. Renata is beginning to understand the experience of not feeling at home. Not feeling at home is like feeling entirely lost. She recently went to a new city where she knew no one, consequently she felt no connection with the world at all and wondered where she was, what was happening. But once she reminded herself that she is familiar with coping in unfamiliar cities, an embryonic level of familiarity was reintroduced, and she was able to manage[14]. The scale of a city impacts Renata's ability to feel 'at home' there. Large cities offer anonymity and the liberation of *having* to accept that they cannot be totally grasped and conquered, while smaller cities remind Renata of her own hometown and this brings the associated burdens of more personal meaning including the fear of judgement. In London, Renata feels there are many other individual strangers like herself so even when walking alone through the city she is in the company of other similar individuals. Again we have this uncanny mix of the familiar and the unfamiliar, the need for some connection and acquaintance but a concurrent need for freedom and anonymity.

For Rita, the feeling of being at home comes upon her in specific kinds of localities rather than being commensurate with having a personal private space. She feels 'at home' in various communities in the world wherever she is able to communicate in local dialects and navigate local life. Rita feels at home when she stands out a bit, though if this generates invasive attention or too fixed an identity, it can feel stifling. Rita's houses in London and in Africa are her homes, both being in very diverse cosmopolitan areas. The importance of a home place is that it gives an independent origin to come back to, a modest settled base in the world, making it easier to venture out and explore.

Despite establishing her own 'homes', Rita's childhood possessions remain in her mother's house and when abroad she has had distressing dreams of her parents leaving this house with all her things inside.

---

14. In the midst of *total* unfamiliarity a degree of familiarity may feel welcome – especially when travelling alone and unsupported, which is characteristic of the journeys of existential migrants.

This dream seems to signifying the continuing metaphoric importance of this place in her life, though she would never consider moving back there. Her adult life continues distant from the stifling little Britain she grew up in and she could never return to that.

Realizing the importance of familiarity to the sense of home can generate a desire to return to one's original homeland. Aging and its associated shifts in what feels important, including inclinations towards increased stability, influence this desire. To return home after years of living as a foreigner implies bringing back some of the personal development that has occurred while abroad and merging that with the home environment. Each participant who contemplates return struggles with how to address the original issues that contributed to the decision to leave. Some suggest the possibility of living in a *cosmopolitan* way in one's own native country, living as an anthropologist lives when studying the rituals of a foreign culture, a mélange of strange and familiar, a home on stilts.

For Eva, after many years of dutiful trips home, she has suddenly begun to enjoy these returns and this seems connected to the different priorities associated with maturing. This shift presents new possibilities for improving family relationships yet Eva also mentions the uncanny sense of visiting home and being confronted by the reality that people have died during her years away and she needs to integrate these 'absent connections' into her own life somehow. Without comprehending it fully, Eva is beginning to feel the clichéd desire to end her days in her home country. It can feel confusing when the impetus to return begins to arise after being away so long. Eva feels that this desire for return has a deep existential or mystical element to it. It holds the promise of deep reunion and *total* belonging by returning to one's origins, a need for real mothering that cannot be provided for oneself, mothering in the broadest sense, being mothered by one's home country. Eva imagines that her growing desire to return encompasses a need to heal the wounds of being human.

Francois realizes that he could not return to his home city and pick up as the same person he was in the past, he has been changed by all he's experienced and the places he's lived in the interim. Despite difficult homeless years, Francois has decided to settle in his London flat and begin to commit himself to study and work here. He has decided that it is possible to have a sense of home in a place that is not the home of one's dreams, while not giving up on realizing those dreams. At certain times, with certain people and in certain places, Francois is able to feel at the centre of his life, and choosing his own life direction has been an important part of finally achieving a modicum of feeling at home in the world.

Some people say 'I can be at home anywhere because I am at home in myself'. Camilla has come to accept that the idealized notion of 'being at home in oneself' is more a slogan than a reality as it necessitates working through deep and long-standing personal issues. Living in an unfamiliar context has allowed Camilla to discern what is really her and what is context-specific, thus unravelling what is essential from what is environmentally contingent. Camilla mistakenly thought that external approval would give her the degree of self-acceptance necessary to be 'at home' with herself. She assumed that the group's acceptance, especially a group of very exacting local peers, would reassure her that she is OK. This infused so much pressure into being accepted that the strategy undermined itself and acceptance became impossible. Camilla optimistically dreams of feeling 'at home' in herself since it would allow her to take that feeling anywhere and therefore to be free. Other participants seemed less optimistic that being-at-home was achievable at all, let alone a portable feast.

Carl left home four years ago and severed his feeling for that place, deciding he'd start over again and never return. However, Carl finds it difficult to make a home in England because the historical context of his childhood is not shared with anyone here. He can't partake in discussions about childhood TV shows and other past cultural references. It is painful to realize he lacks those deep associative roots yet he believes London can become a home in a temporary sense. Like Camilla, a part of Carl's process of re-creating his sense of home and reinventing himself, is based on discerning what is essential to him and what was imbued from his original culture. His life in London has taught him that *ultimate truths* about the world are only *contextual truths* and useless in different environments. He has been in a process of trying to let his new habitat become his new home, including building a new network of social support. Like most of the participants, Carl finds he relates more readily to other foreigners because they share a profound commonality of experience that connects them. Like other outsiders he's had to put effort into learning how each society functions for those on the inside and what their attitudes are towards those like himself who live on the margins.

Carl describes the meaning of home as a place where he can be metaphorically naked, vulnerable, a place that allows both the beauty and the pain of life. This is why his parents' home can no longer be home for him, as their views do not acknowledge pain as a part of life. Anywhere Carl lives must include a space where he can be in solitude for a few hours each week. This is experienced as sacred time, as important as his relationships. This quiet space has replaced his previous religious belief. It is also crucial for Carl that he lives with people who share common values and experiences, especially the experience of being different. Leaving home has been a growth experience for Carl and the learning has been mostly positive. He now knows that in order to adapt he must combine flexibility with the solid grounding of a home base. He is concerned that if he moves too much he might lose the latter and end up without any roots at all. He is intrigued by the fact that he feels more at home in a multicultural area of London, where there is no overriding identity, than in his original home. Carl feels life is so utterly diverse that it could be argued that there's no such place as home - it's all contextual. However in practice Carl admits that he cannot construct home arbitrarily, he can't just decide where he will feel at home, there are certain necessary conditions, including freedom from having to conform and compromise himself.

Although travel has exposed Sarah to people she would never have encountered at home, her first *chosen* friendships retain a special deep significance for her. This is one instance in which Sarah's home culture remains her 'default position'. Sarah still assumes a deep commonality with fellow nationals and she feels relief in the company of people from her home culture. For example, the personal space between people is negotiated in a familiar and safe way, so she can concentrate on just being herself. However, this familiarity with home lessens as she becomes more comfortable in London. Sarah realizes that she is becoming more English and she now makes distinct observations about her home culture: there is a pressure to conform, a condoned form of intrusiveness, characteristics she used to take for granted are now standing out as startling. Though she still feels more relaxed at home, Sarah says 'me isn't me anymore back home' because she's lived so long in London. There's a slippage of one place into the other, and she finds herself in a twilight zone where it's often not clear which world a specific association, expression, or even a certain person, originates from. When she visits home, it is no longer clear whether the misunderstandings between her and locals are due to the years away or because she is mistakenly referencing something that belongs to her London reality.

Sarah notices that 'home is always where I'm not'. In her hometown she says home is London and in London she says home is her hometown, at her parents' country place home is the city and in the city she might call her parents' place home. Sarah says that somehow this ties into the sense of always wanting to be different when she was growing up, but different in a safe and acceptable way. Being able to proclaim, "I'm from somewhere else", introduces uniqueness for Sarah, and possibly distances her from whatever happens where she is. Sarah can overlook negative aspects of her home culture because she is just visiting, but this would be different if she was considering re-settling there. It is much easier for Sarah to visit home as long as the question of returning to live there is not open for consideration. She admits that she thinks a lot about returning short-term but it is never a consideration to move back permanently, and this clarity makes it easier to navigate her visits home.

Sarah knows she will never quite fit in anywhere now, neither in London nor back home. During an extended visit to her homeland, for the first time ever Sarah got homesick for London, which felt exciting because it meant she could finally have that balance of loving her country but accepting living as a foreigner in London. Finally it was OK to accept the difference without comparing the two places.

Two of the interviewees emphasized the importance of their childhood *house* in their feelings about home. Both these people come from a part of the world that has recently been at war. Renata feels the house represents a more innocent and ideal state, a fantasy of happy childhood, when the family was a whole unit with no inkling that it would ever change. Knowing that the house is there has always grounded something in her. The house evokes deep feelings and any changes in its structure are resisted, as though it is a museum and not a living place. It seems that none of her family has achieved separation from that house; it retains an emotional grip over the entire family nexus, especially the females as it has always been passed along matrilineal lines. Renata would contemplate buying the house if possible, to maintain it as it is. If the house was gone, she feels she would lose her homeland; the ground would be pulled from under her, regardless of having no intention of ever occupying that ground again.

It is not surprising then that the shifting boundaries and new national identities of civil war were distressing for Renata, generating questions about what is home, where is home, and the stability of home. She believes that the intense emotional importance of home in national psyches was a catalyst for the war. For her family the conflict impacted upon their physical property, destroying it and disputing ownership, and this was very anxiety provoking. The war in Renata's country lead to the eventual selling of their summer house which she found very difficult as it was the place of many childhood vacations and next to the family home, provided a reassuring physical orientation in her home country. This is reminiscent of the expressed need from other participants for a 'home base'. Changes in physical places can be unsettling in a way that generates personal insecurity. For Renata, that property signified a continuing bond and now that bond is physically severed.

Marta expressed deep emotion in response to the question of returning home. She was reminded of how pleasant her life had been at home, how even twelve years later birdsong reminds her of those peaceful past mornings. Yet she feels she'd be lost there now, everything would be strange again as it was when she first arrived in London. Marta anticipates returning home would be very difficult, she would feel unwelcome, all doors would be shut to her, she wouldn't be able to navigate the society or even the language. Who would she be? Although the thought of returning occurs to Marta, she always rejects it because it would feel like retiring from life. If she returned she'd feel dead. There's nothing left for her there. This constitutes a strong motivation for staying away, it means staying alive, vibrant. When Marta imagines returning to her home culture it is intricately linked to returning to an isolated life with her mother in their big house. Even if she imagines returning after her mother has died, Marta sees herself enclosed in that house, like a prison. As with Renata, but in a very different sense, the house looms large in the life of the family. For Marta, the house remains inseparable from memories of the struggles with her mother and every time she enters the house that atmosphere descends upon her. There is a very strong tie to the house and to her mother, a bond, but not an attraction. She feels drawn to visiting the place but would never stay. Marta resists that imploding world when she visits home, and this resistance causes aggressive confrontations with her mother.

The parents' attitude towards the family locale has an impact upon the child's experience of that place as home. For example, Patricia describes her parents as being unhappy and rootless due to relocation from the country to the city and their rejection of the city as homeworld had an impact on her ability to call the city home. If the parent/extended family rejects where the child is raised, then the child is alienated from the only source of home given to them - the parent's abandoned home was never the child's. The child is denied belonging to their known environment but also does not belong to the historical parental environment; they feel foreign in both places. Not knowing where one is supposed to belong can result in a confused identity. However some children react to this 'homelessness' with *a lightness of place* that allows them to more easily escape the orbit of the family home. Not having a set identity associated to a particular place may allow for increased freedom in choosing who one will be, trying on various identities and places and amalgamating them creatively.

Thoughts of returning home can still generate fear, panic, and anticipated suffocation for some people. However, for others, leaving always implied the eventual return and some participants are already engaged in that process of 'homecoming'. Fiona's overall direction has always been back towards home, though the route has turned out to be rather circuitous and there's still hesitation that return might encompass feelings of entrapment and cultural restrictions. Fiona compares the process to rock climbing, where one takes deliberate and cautious steps and then tests to see if they will hold. She has attempted and then aborted one move back and felt the danger and ambivalence of that. Returning has become a highly conscious and analyzed event due to the deep importance of it. She has never felt she has the right to claim a home in any other place on earth. She could only make that claim in her country of origin; so returning to examine whether it *could* feel like home now has a crucial significance. Fiona did not want a nostalgic ex-pat relation to her homeland. She needs to feel her connection to the place; to really test whether the *concept* of home is real, if it can actually exist. In exploring whether home can be both a geographical and a psychological reality, she is emphasizing the sense of connection, the interaction between self and place, more than the place itself. This requires retuning and working through life stages that were not addressed earlier. Thereby, gaining psychological development from 'homecoming' is a way of having both a sense of home and a sense of moving forward, of personal change. Fiona needs to combine these two sensitivities, to feel she can change what is not satisfactory in the environment in order to settle. She is aware that the reality will be complex, that there will be challenging limitations like those that motivated her to leave in the first place. Also, her worldly life experiences have made her different now, necessitating awareness of how she will fit in and not fit in, situation by situation. She knows she is not going back in time to the original sense of home and she is also cognizant of the fact that she will be returning to a community that most people have never left and there could be resentment and resistance to her return and to her need for engagement.

Peter has also recently returned to his homeland after years of being abroad. Though emotionally difficult, returning home has become an opportunity to reflect upon his time away and the significance of the rite of passage initiated by leaving home. In returning, Peter no longer feels the need to escape his parent's lack of understanding by leaving his home country, but he does imagine his life will always entail travel or living overseas. Peter's time in Asia was transformative and he maintains strong relationships there. Asia has become substantially familiar while remaining forever foreign, therefore satisfying the need for mystery while also feeling 'familiar', perhaps the only place on earth which satisfies Peter in this way. Negotiating unfamiliar and strange situations in Asia proves conclusively to Peter that he can cope in such extremes, instilling in him an appreciation for his own mysterious qualities. It is hard to fathom the uncanny process that has brought Peter to where he is in his life, nonetheless there appears to be a perceptible pattern and although not premeditated or planned, his life seems to express his sense of who he is.

In an inversion of existential migration, Kumar, an 'involuntary migrant' is trying to reconstruct a relationship to his native country, which his parents took him away from at the age of five. When asked about home, Kumar says he uses the word 'home' in two ways, his physical home is in England but his 'real' home is his ancestral home. He is tempted to call his home country his 'spiritual home' and when I suggest that his soul feels at home there, he sighs deeply in agreement. His identity seemingly formed around his native home, saturating it with a special quality that his home in England can never have. England is just where he lives. Kumar experiences his longing for his home country as a positive yearning, whether it is fulfilled or not, though he believes he will relocate there eventually. Not surprisingly, Kumar has wondered what his life might have been like if his parents had not taken him to England as a young boy. He describes the imagined life he didn't have as less complex, simpler, and slower than his life here. As he imagines this unlived life, he considers that his ideal would be to live half of the year in each place. These sentiments echo the desires of many of the other participants and as mentioned earlier it is difficult not to consider that in Kumar we are witnessing the birth of an 'existential migrant' and the homelessness it entails.

When we reflect on these stories and feelings about home, a striking commonality seems to emerge. It is as if 'home' is not simply a 'place' but in fact an *interaction* between each individual and their environment, whether that resonance is momentary, temporary, or long-lasting and durable. This section on 'home' incorporates many of the previous themes of independence, space, and affinity to the foreign, while introducing more explicitly the needs for deep connection, familiarity, and a secure base that is nourishing without being oppressive. It also hints at some of the deeper feelings of nostalgia and loss. For a number of the participants there was an explicit desire for the home country to remain unchanged, like a museum or shrine from the time of one's childhood. There can be considerable distress about the changes in the home country while living abroad. At times of loneliness and crisis there are increased feelings of homesickness and even thoughts of returning, but returning to a place unchanged over the years, in fact a desire for a kind of *time travel*. Going back to just the way it *was*, going back in time. Visits home can cause a turmoil of mixed feelings about the decision to leave and regrets about 'the unlived life' as if it waits for them in an inaccessible parallel universe. However, despite all the unexpected difficulties and paradoxes, *all* those who chose to leave feel certain that given a second chance they would *have to go* again. This certainty is remarkable, given the degree of painful nostalgia, sorrow, and longing that results from having left.

In terms of returning home, I need to confess the extent to which living with this topic has impacted upon my own process of 'existential migration'. Like my participants, my understanding and experience has been carried along by contemplating so explicitly the story of my leaving and being away. My own feelings about 'return' evolved during this project to the extent that after eighteen years away I began to plan my return home to Canada. In fact for me the completion of this research culminated in the sacrament of homecoming, literally a 'rite of passage'. The call that led me away called for my return – but 'return' is misleading. My homecoming was not a reversal but continuing forward with the adventure that began for me long ago in a small prairie town. As mentioned earlier, this return was fascinating and emotional, lasting eighteen months before the call from beyond lead me once again to the departure gates.

In Summary:
Even those people who never really experienced an ideal home environment could describe what that feeling would consist of for them – a place to be oneself, a place to really relax, a source of nourishment and spacious security. 'Home' was also conceived as an interaction, a moment when the individual and the environment 'matched' in specific and idiosyncratic ways, allowing the feeling of being 'at home'. The participants often try to live in two different localities, never achieving 'home' in either but often assigning the term 'home' to the place where one is not rather than the place one actually is. Feeling at home thereby becomes intertwined with a feeling of being not-at-home. All participants had strong emotions about 'return'; longing, fear, or indecision. No one was indifferent to the issue. Feelings about returning home seem to increase as the migrant and their people back home age. Returning home to settle seems to be as much a psychological and philosophical process of healing as a geographical process of relocation. The longer one remains away from home the less concrete seems the experience of home. For many this process culminates in the person not really feeling at home anywhere. Though there seems to be a desire for the home country to remain frozen in time and unchanging, unavoidable change means that home also becomes a foreign country, while simultaneously deeply familiar (stranger in a familiar land). It is interesting that regardless of the emotional pain and losses inherent in leaving home to live in a foreign land, no one would choose differently if they had the choice again. Everyone would leave despite knowing the years of deep difficulties ahead and the inherent irredeemable losses.

6.8 THE DRAMA AND PARADOX OF LEAVING

In this chapter we see how people narrate their own story of leaving, giving detailed 'personal introspections' of their experiences over the years, that wider perspective capturing the drama of 'existential migration'. Throughout these accounts *it is crucial to note that the need to leave home and the reasons given later for leaving can be related without conflating one to the other*. In most cases there clearly exists *an underlying and unfathomed inevitability* about leaving that is never fully explained by reasons that are identified post hoc.

Many leavings were being prepared for already in early childhood. Many participants can clearly discern that they made choices that would facilitate living in other parts of the world even before they could articulate it as their destiny. Learning a foreign language, reading books about foreign places, watching foreign films, can all help to prepare, in imagination, the act of migrating and expectations of future foreign experiences. Holidays abroad can constitute a secretive imaginary 'dry run' of the eventual migration. Leaving the country can seem so important that nothing is left to chance; one must ensure that nothing prevents it from happening.

On the one hand Peter was desperate to leave, feeling alienated and unhappy at home but he was also nervous and anxious about leaving. Fantasies of leaving helped him cope with his home environment and he was concerned that if he couldn't survive out there how could he return and cope at home with that fantasy in tatters? Peter felt the only way he could really leave was to go alone, without anyone's support, as a baptism of fire. Once Peter left and realized he could cope, there was no desire to return home. Peter's choice to study anthropology combined the chance to deeply explore life while living it, to analyze the experience of being alien while being in an alien place. Peter's scholarship also enhanced his tools of observation enabling a return to his origin with a new perspective on the benefits of feeling foreign in his home environment.

For Rita, as for many of the participants, going to university provided the initial excuse and first experience of leaving home. In her case, it offered the opportunity to escape the mismatch between her values and the conservative ethos of her hometown, to abandon arid conventionality and to blossom intellectually. Although Rita had friends who also left for university, a number of them returned after studying, and their original leaving lacked Rita's greater enthusiasm. But it was surprising for Rita to discover that leaving doesn't happen all at once; there was a gradual process of separation from parents and the family home. She was surprised to feel a pang of emotion when she would visit home and then leave again; that same home environment that she despised still retained some emotional hold.

Renata's account of leaving home reveals more of the contradictory and complicated paradoxes in this choice. Recounting it feels very intimate to her, a very private story of gradually moving further and further away from all that one knows. Renata experienced her leaving as traumatic at each stage but most difficult was a period when, for financial reasons, she had to take a step backwards and briefly return to her hometown after having left. Again, pursuing her university degree was a useful rationale, or even excuse, for leaving home. For Renata, the process of leaving expressed her need for increased independence in the form of increasing physical distance from family and home. Like some others, Renata wasn't always conscious that she'd leave home, but it was always implied because from the start she could never imagine staying in her hometown.

Renata felt herself gradually outgrow each space she was in: her room, her parents' house, her own flat, her hometown and finally, her homeland. She reports that this progression of needing to become 'physically bigger' changed every aspect of her life. Like Peter, Renata draws a distinction between all the reasons for leaving and the unmistakable feeling that she just had to go, despite any rationale or explanation. She was not trying to escape from something, but rather was going *towards* something, a curiosity and a search for what she wanted in life, always towards greater independence and self-support. Although Renata clearly felt the need to go, she had no destination in mind and she found that attractive, to just follow the 'call without content'. 'There was a constant compromise between managing her studies and her continual moving; she saw both as educational. Renata knew it would not be right for her to remain in her hometown to attend university; she needed geographical movement to match the intellectual movement. The connection between the realms of abstract intellect and concrete geography produces a deeper appreciation of the knowledge acquired. One's holistic being is more engaged if knowledge is lived in motion than when sitting and reading sedentary in a chair. For example, seeing an exhibition away from home makes it a whole adventure, a whole process that is much more than just the exhibition itself and certainly more than seeing it around the corner from one's home.

However, leaving incurs an inevitable price and Renata is clear about this. When she allows herself to think about leaving behind the loved place she is flooded with a feeling of melancholia. The difficulty is leaving something that one loves, *the place of lack was/is also the loved place* but the loss is balanced by positive excitement about the unexplored. Renata feels comfortable as a stranger amongst strangers, but she also misses the taken-for-granted world at home; nothing functions automatically when you're a stranger. She misses the social network that accumulates over years in the home place, whether one frequently meets with others or not, its existence provides a feeling of bedrock. Though it can feel suffocating to have that network, not having it evokes the longing for it, and Renata is slightly embarrassed to recognize that neither situation, having it or not having it, seems totally satisfying. For Renata, also, the best resolution to this experience seems to consist in having two worlds or easy access to being away and returning home, but the distance between the UK and home is too great to combine them easily and Renata feels increasingly disappointed when she returns home at infrequent intervals and finds things changed; she is losing the world she goes back to find. At this point in her life, Renata is confused about which country to call home and she uses the two languages to signify the home she is referring to, by saying the word in her native tongue or in English. As described by Sarah, when Renata is in one place the other place feels like home, and this mixed identity is now also reflected in her native first name and English surname, each reflecting one of the two places, so she is half here and half there even in name.

Renata constantly plots her homecoming but wonders if it is at all realistic or just a fantasy to quieten her homesickness. She is caught, unable to decide whether to encourage the feeling that there's no place like home, or whether she should try to deny it, which is her usual strategy. Her flat in London consists of unpacked boxes, which reassures her that she could leave at a moment's notice. The price of this unsettledness is that she also lives with persistent anxiety. However, Renata anticipates a new phase, where moving back or not, or going back and forth, are no longer the correct terms. Though unclear, the issue of home seems to be reframed into the dilemma of combining both excitement and peace within one life. She sees the dilemma as having been *'relocated'* from the geographical to the psychological, or existential.

Fiona was desperate to experience what the wider world might offer in sharp contrast to her own local habitat. She was powerfully attracted to the unknown and meticulously planned the steps of her leaving. She has enjoyed her adventures out in the world, describing the process as twofold, geographical and psychological. She regrets not being able to achieve her goals less painfully and she continues to feel detached since returning to the UK.

Graciella left her home country as soon as she possibly could. She wanted to prove to her boyfriend, her parents, and to herself that she could do it. She resisted family attempts to influence her future, opting to leave for America even though she didn't speak a word of English. Graciella's wanted to be out in that wide world, to be in airports, catching flights to exotic new places. But there is also a poignant and powerful image of loss in Graciella's story. She found a newborn sick kitten on her porch shortly before leaving her country. Graciella nursed this kitten and mothered it till it recovered and thrived. She often still dreams of that baby kitten now, dreaming that it's ill and Graciella is not there to take care of it. Though the animal is now grown and healthy, it always appears as small and helpless in the dreams. Graciella feels the kitten symbolizes something she had to sacrifice in order to go away, something she had to leave behind. This is not the expression of simple regret since Graciella clearly values the unimaginable variety of experiences she has had since leaving. But the satisfaction of exploration is beginning to transmute into a nascent longing to be able to return home as a self-sufficient woman. Returning in this manner would soothe something in her, perhaps addressing the poignant need expressed in her dream.

In Sarah's country it is customary for young people to travel abroad for a year and then return home. She followed this custom (or utilized it) but with important variations. For instance, Sarah purposefully chose work that she could easily continue abroad, and then she left with a one-way ticket. Unlike her compatriots, she was preparing to be away without a time limit for returning. For Sarah it was important that she leave home when she felt positive about it and if she returned, it should also be a choice, not due to lack of work or some misfortune. She wanted to maintain her loving connection to her home city but eventually Sarah had to declare that in fact she was *living* abroad, rather than just prolonging a holiday. The meaning of this declaration and the powerful attraction of travelling to exotic places remain mysterious to Sarah. Many of Sarah's school friends have visited her in London and cannot understand her decision to live here rather than the relaxed life in her beautiful home country.

Marta's mother sent her on a training course in London and Marta took this situation into her own hands and decided to stay. She did what she could to make her temporary status here permanent. Marta feels natives underestimate the difficulties of being a foreigner, especially how difficult it is being unfamiliar with each little nuance of a place. Only now, after twelve years, does Marta feel she has enough information to navigate her new culture, but even now she feels it's difficult to push life forward with the same momentum she would have had at home.

For years Eva prepared excitedly for her migration to the UK, studying English and business management to support the move. However, upon arrival unexpected obstacles, including host reactions to her foreignness and intense feelings of not belonging, made the transition seem insurmountable. When the hoped-for new life did not materialize it lead to depression and thoughts of returning home. But things had already changed back home, leaving her marooned between two worlds, *suspended between nations* with no sense of belonging in either. In spite of everything, there is absolutely no regret about leaving. Eva speaks for many of the participants when she describes how feedback from family back home reinforces the degree she has developed while living abroad. *Home is like a reflecting mirror.* Others can react positively or negatively to these changes and the gap continues to increase between the one who left and the ones who stay behind as they change at different rates and in interaction with different contexts.

When Ben first came to Europe he felt he would never return to his home country to live and he continues to feel this way. He describes his experiences since leaving home as up and down, with the beginning of his travels feeling 'euphoric', followed by a growing feeling that he should settle down and take on 'adult' responsibilities.

The focus in Ben's life has shifted to what he feels are age-appropriate expectations - travel for its own sake is no longer as attractive as it once was. In this, Ben echoes changes related to aging described by Sarah, Graciella, Eva, Renata, and others. These changes are expressed variously as trying to 'really settle' in the foreign place or thoughts of resettling at home, either decision laced with assumptions of a more 'mature' way of being. For Ben the converse of the attraction to travel has become the pride of fitting into a foreign culture. He enjoys being treated like a local in London rather than as a foreigner. Though he remains ambivalent about this familiarity, he reminds himself of the loneliness of solitary travel, which he easily forgets when he's settled and romanticizing adventure. However, the paradox is that loneliness is an integral aspect of travel for Ben, it's intrinsic to the act, and travelling with a companion would destroy that essential experience. It seems that Ben's choices revolve around solitude/travel and community/settlement, increasingly complicated by his assumptions about age-appropriate lifestyles.

Ben feels he'd be foolish to give up the things he has developed through staying put, namely a personal relationship and professional career, in order to acquiesce to his desire for adventure. Ben attributes the decision to stay in one place to maturing and valuing the things older people enjoy in contrast to his youthful pleasures. To continue travelling at his current age would need explication – it could signify a fear of growing up and accepting adult responsibility. Ben values both solitude and community, and realizes that while settling for frequent European holidays keeps him from giving up everything, it doesn't seem satisfying enough. On the other hand imagining giving up everything and travelling like he did in his youth also no longer seems quite right. At the moment neither option satisfies completely. He has hopes of developing a compromise by incorporating travel as part of his career. He anticipates that this appropriation of travel would be age-appropriate and responsible, rather than just irresponsibly 'flying away' again. It would be interesting to investigate how many 'existential migrants' are represented in professions that require frequent travel and foreign postings.

Finding employment in an international hotel was instrumental in Martin's leaving, not only financially but also by exposing him to foreign attitudes and behaviour. As evident in many of the participant's narratives, exposure to international culture and foreignness can be inspiring for those who have a predisposition to leave their homeland. Working in a large hotel chain helped Martin develop the confidence to attempt relocation to the UK, to access more of what he had been exposed to. Being able to control his own destiny, rather than have it prescribed, was extremely important to Martin. He was not searching for an easier life but one that allowed more choice and freedom and the possibility of belonging.

The death of a parent or feeling left behind by developments in the lives of friends can loosen attachments so that predispositions to leaving call more clearly. Camilla had not seriously considered leaving her home until a year and a half ago. Her perspective *since* leaving has become more suggestive of what I'm calling 'existential migration'. Camilla used to be afraid of the outside world, feeling she had no idea how to function out there; so being trapped was more comfortable because it was at least familiar. The home situation that Camilla describes could almost be termed '*existential stagnation*'. Camilla had to be assured that leaving home would not mean wallowing in solitary isolation and this is in stark contrast to others who relished the anticipation of solitary adventure. Unlike other participants, for a while Camilla was quite willing to compromise herself at home, adopting views or dressing in ways that were not consistent with her own inclinations. This resulted in a sense of losing herself, culminating in the paradox that the closer she was to being accepted by the culture, the more incompatible she was with herself. She says that she had to sacrifice her 'internal home' in order to belong externally. However, surviving the move to London and coping with change has enabled Camilla to deal with her previous feelings of shame at not fitting in. She is experiencing a new feeling of pride, and an interest in travelling further, living in other places.

After making her move, Camilla feels less oppressed and more alive than she has for years. She feels there are new possibilities for work, training, and relationships. Camilla now realizes that the criteria for belonging to her homogenous home culture was incompatible with the person she knows herself to be. London culture is more heterogeneous and openly diverse, allowing a sense of belonging without being moulded to a narrow view of life. How many others who stay behind would flourish if they had the courage to leave?

If the new country has a culture that seems quite similar to the original culture, the transition was not easier, but in fact surprisingly difficult. It seems that if a culture is entirely foreign, it's allowed to be entirely foreign, but if there is enough similarity between cultures, say for example Canada and Britain, one expects to understand things, and this expectation is often disconfirmed, exposing the depth of difference concealed under superficial similarity. The result is a feeling of disorientation, even panic. It can be difficult to bear these unexpected and subtle differences, to accept that one is actually here, as opposed to back home. In the morass of 'familiar yet strange', one's disturbance elicits the need to grab onto something known and reassuring. Again, we are reminded of the 'unheimlich', the uncanny presence of the unexpectedly strange within the familiar. If the new culture clashes unexpectedly and significantly with the migrant's own cherished values, there can be a pronounced dissonance reminiscent of the sorts of dissonance that inform decisions to leave in the first place, in some cases instigating another 'round' of migration. If 'home' can be understood as an interaction that flows from person-environment 'matching', perhaps feeling 'not-at-home' is the result of an idiosyncratic 'mismatching'.

It would be naïve to suggest that the complicated experience of leaving home, including its complex motives, could be completely understood by anyone. Out of the *holistic weave* of life we might be capable of *lifting out* a few distinct threads but we should remember that these threads never exist distinctly in lived reality. Prima facie this book constitutes an abstract piece of the 'whole' of living experience.

For example, at this preliminary stage, some motivations appear to contradict others, falling into paradox. Many of the participants express the importance of independence, freedom, and choice, on the one hand, while emphasizing the need for approval, acceptance, and belonging *somewhere*, on the other hand. Relationships with other 'internationalists' offers a context within which others can be found who understand the predicament. Being understood as a voluntary migrant, evidenced in these interviews, is deeply valued. Apparent contradictions illustrate the complexity of the experience, as well as the dichotomies that need to be balanced. Living with these competing needs can have unintended consequences, arousing complicated feelings about the limits of human existence.

In addition to the personal development offered in a foreign world, there are often complex reactions to people who have never left their home. While voluntary migrants can feel sadness and sympathy for people who have stayed behind, there can also be a hint of resentment or jealousy, imagining those settled lives as easier because they have not required such resilience and reserves of self-conviction. Coping in foreign places demands an exaggerated degree of self-reliance, potentially leading to isolation, and in turn possibly generating a fragile sense of self. Exposure to other cultures seems to 'open up' *something* that, for some individuals, subsequently complicates efforts to settle back again into the everyday life expected at home. It is a deeply emotional realization that foreign migration can create such a *difference in being* that returning home will not be automatic, and perhaps not even achievable. The homecoming, if it occurs at all, is nothing short of a new migration, never a comfortable reinsertion into the familiar. That idealized 'match' between self and home environment may be forever lost, even in fantasy. And this time the 'mismatch', the failure to feel at-home is the unintended consequences of the migrant's *own choice* to leave, rather than a failure in the original environment.

From the interviews it is clear that the decision to leave the home country was, of course, not apprehended in its full complexity – no one really anticipates the in-between limbo of homelessness. A prime motivation for leaving is to find a place where feeling 'at home' is possible, but the search itself can result in not belonging anywhere, the recognition of which can be devastating. Primary questions of identity surface in the experience of not-belonging anywhere: 'Who do I belong to?' 'Where are my people?' Traversing across nations spawns appreciation for what each has to offer but often the participants report feeling *caught* between the contrasting worlds of two countries; the conflicting feelings are especially difficult when the contrast reveals privileged aspects of the lifestyle forsaken at home in comparison with deprivations in the adopted country. This can generate feelings of inadequacy and shame. Existential migrants, unlike economic migrants, may end up with a lower standard of living as a result of their migration – material betterment is not the prime motive in this process. The lives of friends who have stayed behind evolve according to the prescribed adult patterns, usually including financial and material gains as well as increasing social connections. The comparisons between migrants and those who stay increase in intensity as time passes, with feelings of superiority towards those who settled for the prepackaged life in the home culture. Criticism can mutate into envy of those comfortable lives even though it is clear one could never have survived that choice. Though that settled home life would have been experienced as too constraining, entrapping, and a sacrifice of one's 'true potential', this knowledge doesn't necessarily lessen the lament that one was just too different to live that life.

Kathy's multiple migrations have inducted her children into the experience of being 'global nomads'. Since she and her husband no longer have strong cultural identities, this in-between space has been passed along to her daughters. As a family Kathy sees them as condemned to live in a social-cultural limbo and although she sees this as a phenomenon of the 21st century, she is concerned about how this will affect her children. She hopes they are forging identities that will *exceed* the belonging offered by any one place, thus truly achieving the freedom of nomads. However, realizing the consequences of her lifestyle now, Kathy considers that she could have done things differently, but what? Given that she *had to* leave, what could she have done? Perhaps it is best that she could not foresee the difficulties ahead.

No one in her social circle could comprehend Inez's decision to leave her country and her fiancé, to move to London and learn English. The experience of choosing her own future was so crucial for Inez that she sold her own precious artwork in order to finance the trip. She gave up her whole world and in saying goodbye ultimately understood how important she was to others, but that was not enough to stop her. She packed for her trip a full month before leaving and kept the bag by the door, which she appreciated later was heartbreaking for her mother. Inez sacrificed everything she had in order to pursue a dream that was, for the first time, of her own making.

The skill of adapting to new surroundings is an inherent capability of all the voluntary migrants interviewed. However, a few have pointed out the double-edged aspect of this skill. It is a way of surviving but it also constitutes a threat to remembering who one is. It is a 'dangerous' ability but also an understandable strategy especially when there is no one else to offer support. At those moments feigned belonging may be less painful than remaining on the fringe of a strange new place.

Once Renata feels herself settling into a place she feels an opposite pull to keep looking for 'more'. This keeps her always in a first phase of settling, getting to know a place, surviving, feeling unsettled, settling but needing more, then off again. But now she finds herself increasingly wanting the payoff that could come from staying in one place, achieving new goals by sinking in deeper, maybe having a family. Sometimes she wonders when all this leaving will stop but she has no idea how to satisfy both desires. When she begins to go deeper into a place she always finds stones and eventually has to decide if she should persevere, or if the ground is solid rock and unsustainable. Similar to Renata, the only time Graciella felt she had everything she needed to settle in one place was in Nepal but her spiritual teacher challenged her by saying she could stay and die there or keep moving and live. She now sees that her happiness would not have persisted. Graciella feels that she continues to need the tension of two opposites in order to hold open a space of possibility for herself, as she did with her parents when she was young. She feels she can live as long as she knows that gap is accessible, it provides a refuge if needed. But it remains a mystery how she can actually live this possibility in practical and geographical terms.

Initially Marta began the interview by describing her life as 'charmed' but by the end of the interview she was in tears realizing what a struggle it's been. Now Marta perceives staying away as intricately interwoven with her desire to fulfil her potential. It is important to note that having other significant motivations for migration does not preclude the 'existential' significance of the act. For example, Eva describes both her difficult family situation and economic factors as motivations in leaving home but both these motivations were intimately infused with the primary hope of fulfilling her potential as a person[15]. As a young girl Eva remembers being fascinated with the wrappers on British soap products. To her these colourful packages symbolized a whole imagined world full of promise and potentials that couldn't be actualized in her own culture. Eva points out that voluntary departures can be instilled with great hope, great longing, and deep loss all at once.

---

15. It could be argued that every economic motivation implies an inherent existential motivation – the desire to improve one's status and material conditions is a form of personal fulfilment for some. However, I hope it is apparent that if these are the only underlying attributes of the choice to migrate, then this act is essentially different in kind than the migrations I've been presenting here, which are largely expressions of a desperate need for self-realization beyond simple economic betterment.

A last important note worth mentioning here regards the experience of homesickness – paradoxically it seems possible to feel homesick even when there has been no clear experience of home and no intention of ever returning home[16]. I propose that homesickness is also an 'interactive experience', a comment on the present situation at least as much as a desire for a nostalgic past. Perhaps at bottom homesickness is a forlorn desire for some reconciliation with the givens of existence, the quest for a human form of dwelling that seems offered by life but never actualized.

In Summary:
Some people, even in childhood, begin to make choices consistent with and facilitative of their future destiny to leave. Despite one's desperation, leaving still requires adequate self-confidence regarding abilities to cope in unfamiliar settings. Some participants tested their abilities and planned a phased leaving in order to guarantee that their departure would be successful and they would not be forced to return. Leaving the family home for university or a job abroad was a common first step in incrementally larger migrations, but with the difference of university facilitating leaving rather than leaving facilitating university. These 'existential migrations' have a felt direction to them though not always a clear goal. Economic considerations are not incompatible with deeper motivations for migration – but the more apparent economic rationale can easily mask the deeper process that is simultaneously unfolding, and I would argue is often primary. Despite the unforeseen emotional difficulties of leaving, not one participant regretted their decision in the sense that they would choose differently knowing what they know now.

The skill of being adaptable is necessary to navigate foreign cultures and while this malleability is a positive attribute, it can also threaten one's identity. Comparison with peers and family who stayed behind can elicit complex feelings of superiority and envy. Migrants feel sorry for those who took the

---

16. Also paradoxically, it is possible when visiting home, to not want to stay and not want to leave. This again reveals a tragic dilemma inherent in the limbo of living in-between.

easy route by staying home, but are also jealous of their accomplishments and security. As participants age, some begin to desire the positive attributes of a settled life, while seeking to maintain their mobility and their personal sensitivities. Many participants report being in a limbo state where no place will ever feel like home again. Those who have returned home perceive it as a long and complicated process and by no means one of recapturing what was left behind – there is a melancholic recognition that that life will remain unlived, though in fact it was unliveable anyway.

CHAPTER 7
THE POIGNANT PREDICAMENT

The next chapter attempts to gather together in one description an amalgam of these individual stories of leaving home. It is *one* version. It cannot incorporate all the variations we have witnessed, though my intention is not that. Rather I want to offer a description that's evocative enough that you can form a felt foundation for understanding any version of existential migration. From the preceding accounts of voluntary migration, (migration that was chosen by individuals who could have stayed, at least from an external point of view) we can begin to sense the *felt* experience that has until now remained largely unrecognized. I have presented the description in the next chapter as an illustrative anecdote of the most common features present in the participant stories. I have sent it back to participants for their validation and adjusted it accordingly. This chapter offers some initial comments before the description in Chapter 8 as well as three participant reactions to that description of existential migration:

> Marta: I have now read your description three times and it makes a lot of sense. The bit about longing for home (not your words, but my take on this) is particularly powerful, partly because I don't want to admit this (longing) to myself…
>
> Inez: This is the first time I have attempted to read the description and I had to stop after the end of page three. I felt as if my mind opened, my throat

narrowed and I felt tight down to my heart, and then I noticed I was sitting with a feeling of sadness ... I had unbearable tears ... as I have them now again ... I felt that reading your manuscript put me in touch with my own self – as if I was at home, the home of my body. But this makes me very sad. Where am I going to end up? Where and how am I going to die? The answer is that I don't know how I will ever have a home and this makes me miss people, lovely people that I encountered during my journey. I am thinking right now about my roots and my tears stop and I feel the urgency to go back to my roots and see my family. I realized that I have been 'returning' since last year ... I have been trying to enter into a process of reconciliation where there was originally rejection. Though things have changed I feel there always will be an abyss that is impossible to understand. I can only feel it.

Martin: I was very touched reading the paper. It resonates a lot with my personal experience on a deep level. Also it affected some of my friends who also read it. I liked a lot of things you mention in the paper, for example how my own sensitivities stand out more in a strange environment; feeling stateless and rootless and being torn between two cultures and mentalities; living consciously rather than automatically in the new environment; being treated as more special every time I go back 'home' and so on. I had a strong emotional reaction as I was reading about the homogeneity (I'd call it 'Philistine') and I feel I was actually at risk of being devoured in my original 'homeworld'. And hence migration seemed like a choice between life and death. One aspect that seemed to be underemphasized in your description is the profound sense of loss as one leaves their familiar homeland and throws him/herself into the unknown. For me it meant a loss of security - physical home, family, friends and a familiar way of relating to people. As I came here I had to learn everything new, like a baby who is trying to learn to speak. For me returning is not possible, it would kill all the confidence I have achieved. In terms of homesickness, the greatest loss is mourning the choice I never had – home will always stay a fantasy and never become reality for me.

In places I have used the term 'existential migrant' as shorthand, but I prefer the term existential *migration*. I want to avoid constructing yet another diagnostic category or personal label. I don't think that being an 'existential migrant' constitutes a personality variable, but there may well be individuals who are more likely to engage in 'existential migration' due to their openness to certain sensitivities or potentials in life. This openness may be the outcome of an interaction between their being and their environment, creating a predisposition to this particular act. However, it also seems possible that even these individuals may eventually settle (though what that means may be idiosyncratic), while others who were settled may later 'open up to' existential migration as a strategy for life. People who are relocated through career may find that they unexpectedly become 'unsettled' by the experience of an unfamiliar culture and in response wander for some years before resettling again. This would be an unbidden experience of existential migration accidentally initiated by a relocation that was presumed to be psychologically uneventful. Despite the turbulent economic crises of 2008, 21st century global capitalism will likely continue to require increasing numbers of professionals to leave home at least temporarily and it would be rewarding if this book helped to make some sense of their reactions to these moves.

Existential migration is obviously not primarily an inherited 'trait' if it can arise and subside in virtually anyone in response to his or her changing circumstances. It seems much more like an interactive process, one that may last a few months, a year, a decade, or a lifetime. It also seems that the way that this process begins, and when, may be significant – if one never felt 'at home' at home, leaving may have a different meaning than if one did feel at home for some time and then that belonging became 'dislodged'. And what of the person who doesn't choose for themselves, for example the spouse (so-called 'trailing partner') accompanying their partner's relocation, a person who might never have actively chosen to leave the familiar homeworld? These so-called 'trailing partners' may be forced to confront aspects of existence that otherwise would not have arisen for them. What of refugees, and at the other extreme, what happens to individuals who have a strong affinity for existential migration but do not have the basic freedom, due to economic or political hurdles, to leave? These issues remain substantial questions and with the onset of globalized economies we may find that they require some urgent attention.

I present the description below in the first person, hoping that it will be more evocative if the language is immediate in tone. If the reader can let their attention drop down into the middle area of their body where they typically feel things, perhaps they will notice a feeling begin to form there as they read.

CHAPTER 8
A TALE OF EXISTENTIAL MIGRATION

As soon as 'life' entered my awareness it took the form of a question. Part of my answer was a desperate need to explore the world. This impetus was so self-evident that I remember being shocked to learn that it was not universal. While for me there was a 'call' to venture into the exotic unknown, overriding all other considerations, for many of my friends the road ahead was paved with predetermined expectations. The vague anxiety pushing towards departure further separated me from the familiar settled world I knew. My 'self' feels like an active living entity beyond my own control, deeply informed by this emanating call and its longing for some kind of peace. Migration would be a multifaceted act of self-protection, self-expression, and self-worth: a valuing of my mysterious self, my uncertain life, my being. I am more than what they try to make of me.

I imagine foreign places with alien routines, unknown codes, exciting my unformed and malleable self. I am thrilled by the hoped-for fertile interaction between myself and a new world offering unfamiliar rituals of choice and possibility. It is a relief to see an escape route from the old confining expectations, to be able to defy sameness and to survive. I experience the homeworld as oppressively homogeneous and boring and they expect me to adapt to that in order to fit in. We reject each other – they reject me for not fitting in and I reject them for their narrow pedestrian view of life. How did I end up living here of all places?

The act of leaving creates my freedom and independence, but this step requires enough confidence in myself to think that I can make it out there. I have a greater sense of being able to survive in a foreign and unfamiliar place than at home. Leaving is a choice to survive: If I am not free I am not alive. With my growing confidence I test each step to make sure it will hold and I won't collapse back to the origin. Each leaving has a direction towards increasing distance and difference. The foreign context offers me the perspective to see life as a whole, to look back at my home experience without the danger of being sucked down into that mill of the conventional. I now understand more clearly that I never really was 'at home' in that first world. Feeling different has sensitized me to others' differences, and I find a loose fellowship with other outcasts like myself. Together we enjoy our difference, but we also share the sensitivities that lead us to 'choose' this journey into perpetual 'exile'.

International travel and living as a foreigner in someone else's land are archetypal situations for nurturing a self like mine. But I now come to realize that being rootless also makes me feel insecure and fragile, and it takes a lot of energy just to keep myself from falling apart. I find myself in a kind of indeterminate state, an intangible limbo between solidity and chaos. I no longer know where I belong and sometimes that still excites me but increasingly I feel lost. I look at those who stayed behind and lived the life that was laid out for them, and I feel superior because I had the courage to leave, but increasingly I also feel envious. As time passes, the gap widens and I see their security and the fruit of their deep rootedness increase the distance between us. I realize that a part of me thought I could always return to that life left behind but now I understand it is gone forever. There is no going back through time to the moment of departure – no experiment by which I could assess that alternative settled life.
I think about returning home almost every day. Sometimes I am clear that I would never return, sometimes I fantasize about it, yet other times I feel a dull homesickness, a kind of pull to the only place that could have been home

but never really was. I think this signifies a desire for a kind of spiritual and psychological reconnection, a healing of the self in some way, a reconciliation where originally there was mutual rejection. Return would be a complex process necessitating a melancholic recognition of time: home did not freeze the day I went through the departure gate. Home has changed, though deeply familiar it is also different, and I would return as a stranger in a strangely familiar land. But again, how could I stay and not succumb to the suffocation that led me to leave in the first place? How could I protect my fluid self, elaborated by all my experiences in the world, and withstand the sustained demand to cement into sameness? How can I balance my desire for home with my need for self-direction? Any feeling of being at-home is now forever tinged with feeling not-at-home; the two come inextricably intertwined. Homesickness is a given, not a demand to return home, where the feeling paradoxically continues unabated.

I need to find a balance between the threat of impingement and the arid desert of isolation. I seek deep human companionship without sacrificing the attraction of mobility, change, and fresh stimulation. When I feel myself settling and starting to belong, I relax. But then the opposite impulse for adventure is triggered, the exotic is magnetic and the deepening roots are disturbed once again. I need to live consciously, not automatically. I need to stay awake, to continually 'kick myself alive' so I don't slip into the mundane and habitual. In an unfamiliar culture the everyday demands call for constant attention, there the waking sense of mystery matches my own mysterious self. That was the closest experience I've had to being-at-home, the temporary relief of the world mirroring the mystery of being alive.

What happened back there that I didn't fit in? I can't avoid contemplating that question as I begin to long for the ground to hold me still. Why was it me who left, why not my siblings, my cousins, my peers, most of whom stayed behind unable to comprehend my desperation to leave. My feelings about home and travel cannot be reduced to family dynamics but when I reflect upon my life trajectory it always involves those early years, where the journey originated. From my earliest memories I gazed outward to the horizon and made choices that would facilitate my departure. For me the walls around home did not demarcate where the world ended but where it really began. I knew then that I was different, and they also seemed to know. Feeling different at home was not all painful, I grew to like standing out – and now returning home for visits allows me to feel somewhat exotic, somewhat prodigal, finally with a justification for my difference, but still achingly extraneous to their lives.

My family cannot understand; anyone who chose to stay behind would not comprehend. I sit in silence with a feeling that can't be said, it touches my deepest convictions, hopeful excitement hand-in-hand with irretrievable loss. Sometimes out of a subtle shame I mask my leaving behind economic rationales. But for me the desire was not for riches; it is equally likely that I will end up with less because I left. The imperative was to follow 'potential' as an end in itself, not as a means to material betterment. My migration remains more 'other-worldly' than consumerist. I was called to make manifest an intuitive connection to what lives beyond. But there is also a dawning recognition that one can live only one life no matter how many possible lives one can imagine. After all is said, there is also optimism and satisfaction and some pride from having followed the mysterious path of the unknown with courage, concurrent with a niggling thought that it might actually have taken more courage to stay.

Part Two
A new psychology of leaving home and the advent of global homelessness

PART 2
A NEW PSYCHOLOGY OF LEAVING HOME AND THE ADVENT
OF GLOBAL HOMELESSNESS

Part Two of this book is an attempt to make a bridge between the first person accounts of leaving home in Part One and the usual theories and concepts professionals have developed about migration. I will attempt to describe how everyday and theoretical assumptions about home and belonging are challenged, even inverted, through the lens of this new concept of 'existential migration'. I will compare the participants' experiences from Part One with conventional ideas in order to highlight what existential migration may tell us about life in general. I think that the implications of these lived experiences can inspire our thinking for the world ahead and we will certainly need to begin to think differently if we are to survive the coming decades.

Part Two is comprised of five chapters; the first chapter (Chapter 9) will incorporate major themes of 'self-identity', 'belonging', and the 'meaning of home'. These themes will be compared with contemporary ideas about boundaries, tourism studies, the concept of home, and typical assumptions of migration. The next chapter (Chapter 10) is the most philosophical chapter and revolves around a further discussion of the ideas of Martin Heidegger, and a deeper exploration of home, myths and spirituality, and 'the unheimlich'. Chapter 11 briefly explores practical implications of this book and challenges some common assumptions in areas such as cross-cultural training and work with refugees. Chapter 12 offers a few more comments on the individual psychology of migration and implications for styles of psychotherapy with this population. Chapter 13 compares themes of existential migration with representative accounts from exilic literature and poetry. The book concludes with a few summary comments about the journey of this project, from the rooftop in Calcutta to the writing of this book and a cautionary note about globalization.

CHAPTER 9
SELF-IDENTITY, BELONGING AND HOME

Over one hundred million people moved countries during the first half of the 20th century. At the beginning of the 21st century, international migration has intensified along with the increased flow of goods and capital, all requirements of escalating globalization. But of course migration is not just a recent phenomenon. In the introduction to *Applied Cross-Cultural Psychology*[17], we are reminded that for thousands of years, travellers and explorers, merchants, missionaries, soldiers, legions of social scientists and unidentified others have migrated, travelled, and reacted to the similarities and differences between their own and foreign cultures. 'Culture' refers to the patterns of behaviour passed along from generation to generation, carrying implicit assumptions about life, some of which are typically not questioned until difference is encountered. Culture also refers to less visible aspects of life such as what we consider to be normal, what we value, our attitudes towards life and nature, all of which are imbibed subliminally from birth, to some extent constituting or at least heavily influencing our evolving identities. Members of a community share culture and thereby feel a sense of belonging together through their shared similar identities. Identity and belonging are thereby inherent

---

17. Brislin, 1990

in constituting the experience of 'home', where one comes from, where one belongs because he or she feels 'the same', or as TS Elliot said, 'where they have to take you in'.

It is apparent that what I am calling 'existential migration' is intimately related to personal identity, experiences of belonging, and therefore the experience of being-at-home and not being-at-home. By 'existential' migration I am emphasizing how we create meaning in life, how we create who we will be, how we try to accept what is beyond our understanding while also confronting our limitations, and negotiate all the dilemmas of living in a world with other people. Below I *begin* to explore established ideas from the new perspective of the existential migrant.

9.1 WHAT IS A PERSON?

Migration can be a way to safeguard one's burgeoning identity when the home environment threatens to obstruct the developing self. The foreign place offers a more spacious environment, where personal discovery rather than conformity, is the touchstone for identity formation. Identity is in flux, an interaction of person and place, and while the home environment can suppress one's 'true' identity, having no roots at all can result in a fragile sense of self.

'Identity' refers to how one sees oneself, also incorporating others' perceptions and the way that these impinge upon self-development. My specific interest is about the self-in-migration; what is it that motivates a 'self' to migrate, and what impact does the shift from familiar to foreign environment have upon this project of self-creation?

I will discuss two prominent books, Andreea Ritivoi's[18] *Yesterday's*

---

18. Ritivoi, 2002. Ritivoi is a renowned American cultural theorist, professor of English

Self and Nigel Rapport's[19] *I Am Dynamite*. Both books critique the established opposite views; the postmodern view of a malleable self that can form itself to any culture, and the realist view of a set, permanently fixed, self. These two books offer an in-between conceptualization based explicitly upon migratory experience and partly corroborating the view expressed in the stories in part one. Ritivoi outlines both extremes of the identity debate,

> Realists hold that the identity of a person exists outside a symbolic system, and often try to define it in accordance with an immutable trait. From a realist standpoint, the meaning or existence of the self is not *constructed*, but *given*. Constructivists (or antifoundationalists, or relativists, or postmodernists – the nomenclature varies), on the other hand, point out that the identity of a person is embedded in social or cultural contexts, and that it has no hard core, independent of an interpretive process focused on the respective contexts[20].

The postmodern constructed self is seen as optimistic and hopeful in terms of adaptability in an increasingly borderless world where a malleable person might be advantageous. However, the postmodern view is unable to account for *any* aspect of identity – there is no identity, everything is plastic and arbitrary. Acculturation research depicts migration into a foreign culture as often resulting in profound, usually problematic, repercussions for the individual's sense of self. The fact that immersion into a new culture requires adaptation and adjustment *at all* signifies that *something happens* in this impact, crudely conceptualized in extremes as either assimilation or disorientation. Some kind of 'self' is altered, and if this were not true we'd be hard pressed to account for the lived experience of the participants who leave home to enhance *something* within them. Without some mode of identity *per se*, their migrations would seem arbitrary rather than 'motivated', let alone desperate. The motivations so clearly articulated by the participants require an identity that accounts for this guiding

---

and rhetoric.
19. Rapport, 2003. Rapport is a widely acclaimed writer on migration and identity, and professor of anthropology and philosophy at St. Andrews University, Scotland.
20. Ritivoi, 2002:7-8, *italics in original*

personal impetus (not strictly postmodern) while also considering that the motivation is to actualize one's *potential* by altering the environment (thus not entirely realist). Let's discuss this further.

Displacement from one context to another offers a comparative *difference* and thus an experience of *distance* from taken-for-granted assumptions. This facilitates an ability to contemplate both who I am and how the environment influences me. This contemplation can be troubling because it exposes ordinary life as arbitrarily constructed, it could be structured otherwise – this can result in the 'psychological problems' of migration emphasized in the research literature[21]. However, to redress this tendency to pathology, Rapport suggests that equating displacement with labels such as 'alienation', 'culture shock', 'maladaptation' and 'homelessness' degrades its positive possibilities. These labels give a negative perception of migration as aimlessness, an individual blown incessantly across foreign lands, alienated from their original culture. But this view ignores the human being as making choices, an active agent, *motivated*.

Rapport stresses that the migrant contemplates his or her predicament, making 'displacement a conscious and creative act by which individuals shift and remove and oust themselves... as a route to growth... In displacement lies a route to personal empowerment'[22]. Rapport introduces the term 'life-project' to describe the reflective self that manifests in leaving, providing *direction* more than specific goal. This reveals the individual's 'own authorship' over their life trajectory – not in isolation, but also not solely determined by external culture. In this way, an individual can conceive of new ways of living and question their own identities and the values inherent in their home environment. The emphasis on the active self constructing a life fits well with the descriptions of participants. The participants corroborate

---

21. Aronowitz, 1984; Brislin, 1990; Baker, 1999; Selmer and Shiu, 1999; Leong and Ward, 2000; for example.
22. Rapport, 2003:51

Rapport's celebration of the positive aspects of migration, however, his account seems to underemphasize the equally important sense of loss in their stories.

Andreea Ritivoi also concentrates on the migrant experience, again emphasizing the individual in order to better understand the complexity underlying the generalities of migration. However, whereas Rapport stresses the positive potential for self-creation in displacement, Ritivoi concentrates on experiences such as 'homesickness' and 'nostalgia', revealing that immigrants cannot just be 'born anew' in the new land, nor are they totally self-created.

Like Rapport, Ritivoi acknowledges that identity forms over time, and that adaptation need not undermine our sense of personal identity. However, we also have more public identities in communities where we 'belong', so *who we are* continues to unfurl in these domains of shared sameness and individual difference. She argues that identity forms according to a logic of its own, incorporating what enhances it and dismissing what is inadequate for each person. The self emerges from a 'kernel of identity' that forms the beginning of the person's life story. The self is not an independent object but starts as an unarticulated *sense of what feels important*. This 'sense' is contemplated in solitude wherein we comprehend our motivations, for example to stay or go, or return again. In these quiet moments 'we affirm our awareness that whoever we are is not an existing entity to be spotted and released into being, but a possible search...'[23].

The 'self' is this 'acting upon' and 'responding' to the world. Each cultural crossing elaborates the person, creating a more intricate human being than can be accounted for by any single culture alone. The person begins to exceed any one culture with its set forms of life. This developing complexity means that a person who has lived in two cultures is now 'marginal' to each. Below I have sketched some of the facets of the

---

23. Ritivoi, 2002:169

concept of existential migration that are lifted out by this discussion and which in turn could carry forward our thinking in these areas.

1. The participants make it clear that somehow they have gained enough distance from their environment to reflect upon it. *An identity that stands apart from the home environment predates leaving* and this identity constitutes the self as an active agent, able to contemplate leaving.
2. The individual connects with an inner motivation, or 'call' to realize their potential. It is not clear where this 'call' originates from[24] but it does not seem to emanate from the culture. This idea fits with Ritivoi's description of self as an unarticulated search – having direction rather than content. Thereby the *self is conceived as felt potential* rather than set content or cultural construction.
3. Conventional research into migration emphasizes the challenges of cross-cultural experiences and plays down the potential benefits for the individual in terms of developing a self-reflective life project. The participants' stories balanced the potential and the loss, incorporating the whole ambivalent nature of leaving.
4. Rapport describes the positive consequences of migration. But the participants also stressed the 'desperation' to leave, the 'need' to go. It was not solely a positive choice but also an impulse born of *self-survival as much as self-development*. This choice implies some sense of 'homelessness' or rootlessness, resulting to some extent in a sense of self that is robust and adaptable, while also fragile.
5. By virtue of the complexity that results from cross-cultural elaborations, the migrating individual gains a wider perspective but strangely also becomes *less* able to understand either culture and certainly less likely to identify with either. Cross-cultural experience complicates the person beyond existing cultural forms so that the meeting that occurs between a marginal 'existential migrant' and a native 'homebody' often seems to miss the deeply-rooted, uncomplicated understanding that two native persons have.

---

24. Further exploration of this 'call' recurs in the section on Heidegger's thought.

9.2 BELONGING

We cannot assume that belonging exists 'at home'. Ideally belonging would consist of warm connectedness, incorporating acceptance of one's unique person, a welcoming of diversity. When belonging is conditional upon conforming to an oppressive homogeneous environment, this is an unacceptable sacrifice for individuals who are different or unconventional. Sometimes a kind of belonging without claustrophobia is achieved by living in two places. It is also possible to feel a sense of belonging within a diverse group of fellow internationalists who share implicit similarities. Some measure of settled belonging seems to facilitate more self-development than can easily be achieved in a completely migratory existence.

Belonging[25] could be conceived as a bridging process between 'self' and 'home', and is implied in both. 'To belong' is to possess an identity that is welcomed and accepted, and felt as such. It implies positive experiences that secure an individual's sense of self within a specific group. For many people a sense of belonging seems to offer a bulwark against the contingencies of life. To belong suggests an ability to locate oneself within a reassuring family, locality, religion, nation, or other context of sameness. Belonging, then, is to find, and perhaps to some extent thereby attempt to 'fasten' one's own identity within a larger identity, but which larger identities should one choose? This question reveals that in the participant stories *national* identity is typically the ultimate template for explorations of belonging. The logic that follows from this assumption is that

> ...all individuals *should belong* to a nation and have a *national identity* and state citizenship and that the bordered state sovereignties are the fulfilment of a historical destiny. This view has become pivotal in defining not only our world-views but also human identities'[26].

---

25. Extended discussions of belonging occur in the section on spirituality and philosophy of home.
26. Paasi,1999:69, *italics added*

If *national* belonging is of prime importance what are the ramifications for those of us who are disconnected from national identities, shunning them or at least holding such identities at arms length and with very mixed feelings? More perplexing, what kind of schism is revealed by those individuals who have found greater affinity to a foreign culture and in effect have been 'misidentified' with their original home culture? This seems to suggest some interaction between self-identity and national culture wherein an adequate 'matching' must occur in order to experience belonging, otherwise there is a 'mismatch' and the individual continues to seek a context that will allow their identification to flow. Belonging, like identity, therefore attains the status of constant dynamic process rather than finalized accomplishment.

For the participants, identification with other international migrants presents a kind of belonging based upon diversity. Again highlighting that belonging seems predicated upon some sense of similarity, though this may be based upon implicit similarity of values and outlook rather than visible manifestations of cultural sameness.

Just as borders are in flux, as we've seen in recent re-mappings of the world; the 'belonging' aspects of our identities are also fluid: 'who I am' is in constant relation to *where* I am and *who I am with*. For example I belong to the Canadian 'we' in the foreign 'them' context of London but I lose much of my national identification and become more marginal, 'less Canadian', when I'm in Canada. The concept of existential migration prioritizes the individual point of reference as a stance toward the collective. Such an individual is actively attempting to resolve existential dilemmas such as 'who am I? Where do I belong?'.

Of course being uprooted from a national community does not automatically lead to the loss of one's traditional cultural identity and therefore the loss of belonging. For example, we have all encountered expatriate communities that not only maintain their national identity, but exaggerate it in the foreign land. So, belonging is more like a process defined only *partly* by territory (house, locale, nation). However, there is an obvious bias in the study of society and migration in favour of place. Our ideas of culture and belonging are biased towards the fixed and stable rather than change, migration, and travel. *Implied in this bias is the assumption that the home country of origin is the normal and ideal habitat for its citizens, 'the place where one fits in, lives in peace and has an unproblematic culture and identity'*[27]. According to this scheme, returning home would be unproblematic because it's where a person belongs and feels most safe and secure. This reification of home as a place of comfortable belonging is challenged by stories of existential migration and will be further addressed in the next section.

In *The Needs of Strangers*, Michael Ignatieff argues that after the last century of war and destructive nationalism, the world may be ready to shift the attachments of belonging from national to international objects. In his view, 'Modernity is changing the locus of belonging; our language of attachments limps suspiciously behind…'[28]. Ignatieff points to globalization as evidence that old patterns of belonging are no longer even rational, but in order to shift to a kind of global belonging, he thinks 'Our task is to find a language for our need for belonging which is not just a way of expressing nostalgia, fear, and estrangement from modernity'. Ignatieff offers interesting comments about modern belonging, highlighting more biases in our common sense views,

> We think of belonging as permanence, yet all our homes are transient. Who still lives in the neighbourhood where they grew up? Home is the place we have to leave in order to grow up, to become ourselves. We think of belonging as rootedness in a small familiar place, yet home for most of us is the convulsive arteries of a great city. Our belonging is no longer to something fixed, known and familiar, but to an electric and heartless creature eternally in motion… Perhaps above all we think of belonging as the end of yearning itself, as a state of rest and reconciliation with ourselves beyond need itself. Yet modernity

---

27 Malkki, 1995: 509, *italics added*.
28. Ignatieff, 1984:139.

and insatiability are inseparable... We need to see how we live now and we can only see with words and images which leave us no escape into nostalgia for some other time and place... Without a language adequate to this moment we risk losing ourselves in resignation towards the portion of life which has been allotted to us'[29].

Ignatieff wrote this before the fall of the Iron Curtain, the World Trade Centre attack, the American 'war on terror', and the tumultuous economic crisis of 2008 which revealed that the pace of globalization and westernization has increased to fever pitch. Ignatieff himself is a voluntary migrant, having left his native Canada for London, then moving on to the United States to teach at Harvard and most recently returning to Canada to take a role in *national* politics. It is perhaps impertinent to wonder how his own experiences concerning belonging and impermanence influence the view he espouses above. Contrary to his depiction of the world, 98% of people still do not migrate at all, preferring to settle in permanent or long-inhabited homes and small localities, even within big cities[30]. They make settled permanent lives, presumably even in the 21st century, and the clash with globalization, for most people, will likely occur when international culture begins to seep into their loved neighbourhoods rather than through international travel experiences or corporate relocations. Most people still equate belonging with permanence, reconciliation and place (rightly or wrongly). Perhaps Ignatieff, and existential migrants like myself, represent a minority way of being whose thinking about themselves, including this book, offers us a 'place' of belonging that can't be generalized to the majority, yet. But perhaps that is changing, quickly.

Possibly the modes of belonging Ignatieff reacts against are designed to serve a more profound purpose −to camouflage the very nature of existence itself. If such speculation holds any veracity, devoid of such camouflage we may be entering a more anxious age, one of global not-belonging. More anxious but also more true? Perhaps human

---

29. Ignatieff, 1984:141-2
30. Hammar & Tamas, 1997:1

existence implies particular givens that cannot arbitrarily be bent to the will of modern capitalism. These conjectures are addressed more fully in the next chapter.

This brief discussion of 'belonging' in the context of migration suggests elaborations for the concept of existential migration. These provide some striking contrasts with our usual assumptions and forms of belonging. Below are some of the points lifted out by this discussion.

1. Belonging is not an *automatic state* generated in one's origin but more appropriately conceived as a fluid temporal process, like identity, unfolding in time so that one can belong and not-belong at various times in the same place, and lose and regain a sense of belonging.
2. Belonging can feel claustrophobic, an obliterating demand for conformity.
3. The status of 'belonging' is perplexing in that participants long for it while eschewing its conventional forms in favour of individual, even solitary, quests for self-development.
4. Most participants' identities seemed linked with migration itself; perhaps a person can *belong* to the journey rather than the place.
5. Existential migration presents a stark counterpoint to the modern emphasis on national belonging. National boundaries may function as containment against the insecurity of human life, offering a kind of geographic embrace. For some people this familiar nation-state is an unacceptable imposition upon the potential for individual adventure. Scholarship in the different disciplines concerned with migration will have to take account of existential migration if they are to say anything applicable to the species as a whole.
6. In the dichotomy of 'us' and 'them' our participants quite consistently aligned themselves with 'them', strangers, outcasts, and other marginals like themselves. The kind of difference and the kind of similarity that matters to existential migrants seems different than the settled community.

9.3 CONCEPTIONS OF HOME

'Home' remains an emotionally charged issue for those who leave. Even people who never felt 'at-home' could define home as a positive place to be oneself, a place to really relax, a source of nourishment and security. The solid architecture of the family home, or the illusion of an unchanging homeland, can provide a secure anchor for some individuals as they seek adventure out in the world. 'Home' can be redefined as an interaction, a moment when the individual and the environment 'match' in specific and idiosyncratic ways, temporarily allowing the flow of being 'at home'. The longer one remains away from home the less concrete it becomes. Since the homeland continues to evolve while the person is abroad, the result can be a person who doesn't really feel at home anywhere.

9.3.1 Home as House

Most ideas about home assume *that Human Life takes place within the confines of a settled locale*. It is very easy to automatically equate home with house, often based upon one's own association of childhood house with a feeling of at-homeness. 'In memory, then, our house is a place of *protection* and *security* where we are safe, where we withdraw, and where we find comfort'[31]. Home is often described as the place where we are 'at peace', 'on familiar ground', 'relaxed and comfortable'.

'Home', whatever it is, is without doubt particularly significant for most individuals, but it certainly does not unequivocally possess the features ascribed to it above. Participants in this research have not typically experienced the cozy archetypal abode and the 'authentic communication' typical of the 'homely relations' that constitute a 'true home'[32]. In contrast, these individuals report not feeling at-home in their original house, feeling suffocated rather than cozy, leaving the family habitat in search of the very at-homeness that home didn't

---
31. Baldursson, 2002:2
32. Baldursson, 2002:7

offer them. These exceptions reveal that 'at-homeness' must not be defined solely from the view of the settled and conventional ideal. It must take into account the individuals who desperately leave in search of home, or who feel most at-home in a strange land. The supposition of home as childhood origin represents a ubiquitous bias within most of the literature and research on the significance of home and the experience of migration.

9.3.2 House as a Reflection of Self

In her intriguing text *House as a Mirror of Self – Exploring the Deeper Meaning of Home*, Clare Cooper Marcus investigates the meaning of a house to its inhabitant. In Marcus's view, the relationship between self and dwelling has a 'preverbal' and 'mystical' aspect to it, best expressed in literature and art rather than the work of psychologists, anthropologists, architects and so on. Marcus coins the term 'domocentrism' to describe the 'desperate clinging' to what is inside the home. In this case, she believes that the relationship to the house has become a replacement for relations with other people and the contents of the house are used as a compelling psychological defence against insecurity. Marcus provides interesting accounts of remodelling, hoarding, and other house-centred activities that she sees as attempts to work through past and present psychological difficulties.

Marcus has also conceived the term 'domophobia', supposedly referring to those who find it 'extremely difficult to stay in any one place long enough to feel "at home". Marcus boldly asserts, 'For such individuals, having a permanent abode is fraught with too many unresolved emotional issues from childhood'[33]. The 'domophobe' is supposedly stuck in an emotional state in which security is associated with the vast expanse of the amniotic fluid, rather than the solid object of the mother. Yet, according to Marcus, in order to nurture the soul we may *have to* leave home, live in different places at different times to

---

33. See Marcus, 1995:85-90

facilitate the nuances of emotional development. She believes 'When we start to feel not totally at home in our dwelling or, conversely, when we seek a broader home in another place, it is likely that the soul is demanding recognition'[34].

It is unclear how Marcus would ascertain who among our participants are 'domophobes' and who are seeking 'soul recognition'. The participants express the binaries of 'having to escape' with 'exciting journey of self-discovery', presumably typical of both categories according to Marcus. Though there is crossover between the participant stories and some of Marcus's text, Marcus reifies traditional settled life as the given and as somehow less tragic than the transitory vast expanse of homelessness. Though Marcus offers sensitive and insightful glimpses into the complex relationships we can have with our physical houses, she also reclines into more simplistic causal assumptions of childhood experiences determining our adult choices. Our participants explicitly warned against simplistic causal links with childhood.

In *Returning to Nothing, The Meaning of Lost Places*, the Australian historian Peter Read presents oral histories of his fellow countrymen who have been forced out of their homes, for example by natural disaster, economic necessity, or redevelopment. Read explores many fundamental questions applicable to an understanding of settled life and by implication offers comparisons with the opposite experience of existential migration. By comparing stories of existential migration with his stories of forced evacuation, certain facets of both processes stand out more clearly. Read's text is a beautiful and haunting love song to lost places. In a sense it's a testament to what participants in this study have not had - permanent emotional rootedness to a convincing 'home' place. Read's basic premise is that humans feel some necessity to turn space into place, to erect mental and social boundaries that demarcate certain sites as unique, as 'home'.

---

34. Ibid: 252

Read begins his exploration by posing the question, 'How do humans form such powerful and mysterious attachments to country'? Read's specific interests, though fascinating and certainly worthy, tend to skew his accounts; in order to demonstrate the neglected importance of human attachments to locations, he concretizes place as object. He argues quite convincingly that the sense of 'place' has been given scant attention by western researchers. Though Read consistently maintains the equivalency of home to place, he also recognizes and lists some of the important interactions that may constitute part of the multiplicity that generates that feeling of 'home',

> As well as the space it occupies, people conceptualize their home as the functions it performs. To some, home is a comfortingly bounded enclosed space, defining an 'other' who is outside. Others, more socially attuned to their neighbourhood and friends, see 'home' not as a place but an area, formed out of a particular set of social relations which happen to intersect at the particular location known as 'home'. 'Home' can be a focus of memory, a building, a way of mentally enclosing people of great importance, a reference point for widening circles of significant people and places and a means of protecting valued objects... Home is the ultimate focus of all lost places[35].

After presenting numerous narratives depicting the agony of losing a loved home, Read offers the more perplexing account of 'Con', who 'always felt restless, and at the age of forty had not stayed in any one place longer than four years'. For Con, though he spent most of his life in Australia, his sense of belonging has become 'one of the central uncertainties of his life'. As Con sees it,

> The traditional heritage of a place depends on people believing the same relative notion of what the truth was. I was conscious that I was not sharing it with others, and that other truths were possible[36].

Read assumes that Con's experiences are explained by the fact that his parents are European immigrants who stressed the importance of Australian acculturation but within strong continuing bonds

---

35. Read, 1996:102
36. Read, 1996:44

with their motherland. While it makes perfect sense to think that this may have impacted Con's sensibilities, we still need to ask why only Con developed accordingly while his siblings exhibited no such characteristics. Also, there is no consistent cause-effect outcome for all children of reluctant or homesick immigrants. Though he feels some envy for those who are deeply rooted, Con also feels liberated from the trap of being tied to place. He feels that his weaker rootedness has allowed him to become more self-reliant. He appreciates values of personal freedom and openness, yet also feels sorrow about his lack of connection. If we read Con's own descriptions, it is tempting to ascribe to him a process of existential migration. When Read asks 'Whence arose this profound and ambiguous rootlessness?', it again suggests prioritization of the settled over the transitory, as if being settled is *the given* and rootlessness is an aberration that requires explanation or even diagnosis.

In contrast to Read's population, many existential migrants are not closely attached to any one place, and furthermore are disparaging toward the homely, similar to DH Lawrence in his comments on suburban living[37],

> ... all these little dog kennels – awful piggling suburban place ... Is this all men can do with a new country? Look at those tin cans!... There was something indescribably weary and dreary about it.

Read assumes that such antipathy is explained by the distinction between observer and local inhabitant, 'Suburbia is so familiar to the resident, so unfamiliar to the outsider, so individual to the gardener, so uniform to the critic'. Without disregarding the importance of place to Read's interviewees, from the accounts of existential migrants we can point out that there are also 'outsiders' within the community, living with their gaze averted from the locality that their neighbours love so dearly, instead dreaming of imagined foreign lands far away. Their fences do not mark where home ends but where it *might* really begin.

---

37. Rita's comments on her hometown are a prime example.

Not everyone living in a place, even suburbia, is blindly attached to the place, umbilicalized and in love with the uniform manicured lawns. Since it is clear that a particular unrecognized minority do not form unambiguous attachments to country, it raises questions regarding the status of 'home'.

A salient distinction between my participants and Read's interviewees is that his people mostly described group experiences of movement while the people I spoke with mostly engaged in solitary journeys. The losses Read documents, though deeply personal and distinct from individual to individual, occur within a social nexus that allows them to be publicly recognized and spoken about. Read's text referred to whole neighbourhoods or even entire towns that were dismantled and relocated, or suddenly lost to violent storms. This impresses upon the event a degree of public validation that has been missing in the case of existential migration. For some participants, the research interview constituted the very first *recognition* of their experience. It was their first opportunity, ever, to construct a coherent dialogue around their leaving, even though these issues have remained a constant source of fascination to them. I think this explains to some extent the deep emotion of the interview sessions. The next section explores the group refugee experience, shifting the focus away from the settled as norm.

9.3.3 Home in Forced Migration

In his recent text *Therapeutic Care for Refugees - No Place Like Home*, the clinical psychologist Renos Papadopoulos stresses that people who have been forced to flee their homes are not treated as if home itself was a significant issue for them. This point, and the fact that Papadopoulos equates home with place, is reminiscent of Read's book presented above. However, Papadoupolos also defines home as a territory that *evokes the feeling* of being at home; therefore it is both geographical and psychological. He suggests that there is a foundational substratum to human experience and the 'very fact that one has experience of a home (regardless of how good or bad, long or brief, it may be) forms part of this substratum that contributes to the establishment of a foundation to being human'[38]. This fundamental level of human experience, according to Papadopoulos, only comes into view when it is disturbed, for example in the refugee experience. Papadopoulos concludes that the loss of home constitutes a primary disturbance, which he calls nostalgic disorientation, reminiscent of 'ontological insecurity', 'existential anxiety', 'angst' and 'dread'. The resulting deep absence creates a 'syndrome' of homelessness. Papadopoulos assumes that attachment to a secure home constitutes psychological health while homelessness, or not-being-at-home in the world, is a risk factor associated with psychological disturbance.

Papadopoulos believes that when a home is lost, the psychological containment that it offers breaks open and disintegration can result, on all levels, individual, family, and social. Homecoming nostalgia, in this view, is a desire both for a physical home and for the lost containment; in fact, family and home are treated as inseparable entities. How would Papadopoulos account for the existential migrant's obvious ambivalence regarding home? Our stories do not fit easily within the way he concretizes home as 'holding', implying a reliable stationary *place*. Papadopoulos characterizes home as

> ... a primary condition where one's presence and entitlement are taken for granted. Unquestionably, one does not have to earn the right to be at home. One should not be required to achieve anything to gain the right to be at home. Home is where one is[39].

From their loss of home, Papadopoulos believes that refugees are bound to share a deep 'nostalgic yearning for restoring that very specific type of loss'. *Nostalgia* derives from the Greek *nostos*, which means returning home, and *algos*, which signifies an ache or pain. According to Papadopoulos, this is a unique type of loss, encapsulating

---

38. Papadopoulos, 2002: 17
39. Ibid: 38

a multidimensional signification of the physical, imaginary, psychological, origin and goal, return and reintegration. This powerful mixture of dimensions creates confusion and bewilderment,

> ... most homes provide some kind of continuity that enables co-existence between many opposites: love and discord, distance and proximity, joys and sorrows, hopes and disappointments, flexibility and obstinacy, envy and magnanimity, rivalry and collaboration, loyalty and betrayal, enmity and friendship, similarities and differences, to name but a few... Regardless of how 'dysfunctional' families may be, homes can provide that deep and fundamental sense of space where all these opposites and contradictions can be contained and held together. Inevitably, this develops a sense of security, regardless of whatever other traumatic experiences family members may also have as a result of their family interactions[40].

Papadoupolos offers a helpful description of the devastating expulsion from home suffered *by those who were settled*. However, his analysis does not account for the participants' original lack of belonging at home and the resultant search for home elsewhere. He does not seem to consider that homelessness, like home, may also be a given substratum of human being. In his account home becomes a containing space of bricks and mortar, but not everyone seeks *concrete* containment and the participant narratives suggest an abhorrence of such 'holding'. Proclaiming that we have a 'right to be at home' neglects the question, 'as what'? Prisoner? The participant experiences of home are less equated with place, and certainly more ambiguous, partly due to their experience that their whole self was not welcomed at home – they had a *conditional* right to be at home, earned through conformity. Despite reassurances to the contrary, our participants do not represent home as *the place one is meant to be*, in fact not even as *the place one finds convincing*. One participant described home as where she was 'put to grow up'. Evidently for some, entitlement is not enough to feel at home.

In his paper on Bosnian refugees, Richard Black[41] proposes that

---

40. Ibid: 16-17
41. Black, 2002

simplistic notions of 'home' have contributed to the problems associated with post-war reconstruction. He says the contemporary world is associated with 'a metaphysical loss of home', conveying a lost past which leaves both migrant and refugee longing for a distant inaccessible home, the impossibility of its achievement increasing the strength of identification. Migrants often 'overlay an imagined homecoming on the clear physical impossibility of reaching a fixed and distant geographical place' while policy-makers look at political and economic tensions as the obstacle to return home and do not see the notion of home itself as problematic. Based upon the participant stories, the question arises as to what kind of 'home' is longed for and how is such a home actually experienced if it comes to fruition?

There is a body of theoretical literature on home, but little of it is grounded in what people themselves actually say about their experiences of home and migration. Most of the literature, no matter how nuanced and sophisticated, seems to take as a starting point home-as-place. In a departure from this, Sociologist Dorothy Massey in her text ironically titled 'A Place Called Home' suggests that the *social relations* of 'home' are most important, resulting in localities with fuzzy edges to them, obscuring where one homeworld ends and where another begins. This softening of the assumptions regarding the factors that make up 'home' leads us into the next section, further 'deconstructing' the edifice of home.

9.3.4 Home and 'Migrants of Identity'

In this section we find an understanding of migration that comes much closer to the concept of existential migration. Anthropologists Nigel Rapport and Andrew Dawson in their text *Migrants of Identity* argue that we urgently need a framework to rescue the individual migrant from being inconsequential to understanding migration (or home). We need to think the individual back into a central role within human history. They suggest that we could start by regarding movement not as a deficient interval between the solidities of departure and arrival but as an authentic mode of being in its own right. Rapport and Dawson suggest that it is through the search for identity that an individual defines him or herself and as the search is ongoing, the definition is always unfinished.

These authors present examples such as waiting rooms, refugee camps, transit stations, shopping malls and international hotels, as transit points and 'non-places' arguing that in today's world no place is complete in itself and no place is completely foreign. Movement has become fundamental to modern identity. 'And in this situation, people are always and yet never 'at home': always and never 'at ease with the rhetoric of those with whom they share their lives"[42]. For a world of travellers, labour migrants, exiles, global capitalists, and commuters, home may be found in a routine set of *practices*, in styles of dress and greeting, in memories and myths, in stories carried around in one's head. The authors seem to be blending their descriptions into an almost political project geared toward liquefying the conception of home. Rapport and Dawson suggest that how 'home' is understood provides a useful insight into an individual's 'world view', a unique *constellation* of memory, longing, the ideational, the emotional, the physical, the spatial and the temporal, the local and the global, the positively and the negatively charged.

These authors suggest that migration is a resource in the quest to come to know oneself as much as this is possible. From this perspective 'belonging' also must incorporate a degree of estrangement or alienation from which self-knowledge and awareness emerge. Some participant descriptions corroborate this view by accepting a necessary degree of not-belonging within experiences of 'home', enough displacement to offer distance and space. These are interesting concepts, with striking resonances to Heidegger's thought on homecoming, as we will see later. However, new conceptions of 'belonging' and of 'home' are required

---

42. Auge 1995, c.f. Rapport and Dawson, 1998: 108

'Home', we suggest as a working definition, 'is where one best knows oneself – where 'best' means 'most', even if not always 'happiest' ... One is at home when one inhabits a cognitive environment in which one can undertake the routines of daily life and through which one finds one's identity best mediated – and homeless when such a cognitive environment is eschewed[43].

This contrasts with ideas of being-at-home that assume acceptance and intimate belonging, even the avoidance of difference, and a lack of self-awareness. The formulation above seems to offer a more fluid version of home that is lived in awareness even in the midst of routine. I must point out that this version of home, innovative as it is, seems to deviate slightly from the stories I've offered. Though it comes close to the *interactive* version of home consistent with the concept of existential migration, it also suggests that home could exist anywhere, yet participants have found, quite painfully, that home does not arbitrarily occur, is often temporary, and sometimes occurs when one is least able to navigate daily routines rather than where one is cognitively 'best mediated'. We have seen that some of the participants feel most 'at home' where self and world is mysterious and unfamiliar. However, the definition of home above is at the very least a direct challenge to conventional understandings in which home is equated with a fixed place, stationary and centred.

Rapport and others are beginning to re-conceive 'home' in order to take account of increasing globalization and increasing movement. They talk of a mobile home, home as partly constituted through shared social interactions rather than bonded to place. They suggest both that one can be at home in movement and that movement can be one's home. When we compare this concept to the experiences of the participants, it raises the question of whether home is reduced to just another way of being 'homeless'? Perhaps the emergent concept 'existential migration' is needed to help our current ideas stretch to accommodate the pace of global change.

---

43. Rapport and Dawson, 1998:9-10

It is difficult not to think of home as place but what if this is simply a misleading manifestation of concrete settled thinking? Of course home is *related* to place, and to many things, like relationship, mood, sounds and smells, food and furniture, acceptance, freedom, personal values, and other individual sensitivities. What if 'home' is the name we use for specific interactions in specific environments (familiar places of origin as well as entirely unfamiliar places); interactions that are constantly in flux, constantly developing through new experiences. For every individual it will be a unique 'kind' of interaction that raises, even momentarily, a feeling of being at home, and perhaps a slightly different kind of interaction each time. But it is also unquestionable that there is something shared in these phenomena, something we distinguish and potentially understand when another person talks of 'home', being 'homeless', feeling 'homesick'. Although the participants mostly display conflicted relationships to 'home', these feelings are no less manifestations of 'powerful and mysterious attachments' than the strong sentiments expressed by people who have lead settled lives but by misfortune suddenly lost their beloved place. The strength of the emotions aroused by the participant interviews demonstrate that issues of 'home', 'returning home', 'place' and 'displacement', are deeply evocative and in no way the subject of passing indifference just because one *chooses* to leave.

Based upon the study so far, we can challenge the trends in this thinking even further. Life is not just poured into various empty human bodies that then give it shape. We have seen the participants *interact* and respond to their *given* places in particular ways, but clearly not tied to the conventionally understood deeply-rooted bonds that originate a biography. The interaction between these individuals and their environments shows that for some individuals the *foreign place* feels more like home. Sometimes the unfamiliar context can provide the longed-for interaction 'homing' and it is this *felt* interaction that serves as the *sine qua non* of what is referred to as home, no matter how temporary, no matter where.

Arising from this, I would suggest that our associations to place are not stacked away in some psychic basement waiting to be unpacked when we garner the courage to revisit our childhood home. Rather, those first experiences, and their reverberations, are continuously implied in every place we visit, whether the interaction between self and place makes them felt or not. A strange market in Cairo may provide exactly the 'momentary match' that allows some of those interactions to unexpectedly flow again, and we utter in the midst of this foreign bustle, 'It's so strange, I feel I know this place, this is great, I feel peaceful and it's exciting, I feel comfortable, *I feel I could live here...*' And by 'here' we mean the experience of this moment, not this market. An experience of 'home' arises and flows and eventually recedes. Is that moment any less 'home' than the little house where we originally played games and learned about the world? For some of us Cairo might feel more like home while the childhood home alienates in a unique and special way.

Perhaps cross-cultural elaborations can complicate an individual to the point that he or she becomes increasingly unlikely to find any body-environment 'match' will allow the feeling of being at home. Perhaps there are not many social or physical environments complex enough to 'match' an increasingly elaborated cross-cultural person? If this is at all true, then we may begin to consider the implication that *the sort of complexity experienced by cross-cultural people inevitably generates a kind of unheimlich sense*, a not quite fitting-in anywhere. What does this mean for a world that is increasingly demanding that we become cross-cultural, global, citizens? Perhaps we are witnessing the end of belonging, at least belonging of a certain kind.

Below are a few other points from the discussion on home:

1. 'Home' cannot be abstracted from the experiencing individual involved. This implies that national borders constitute 'false boundaries on the free wanderings of the 'homeless' cosmopolitan

mind'[44].

2. 'Home' can refer to one's *origin* and to the *feeling of being-at-home*, and contrary to most expectations, one cannot be reduced to the other.
3. It is important to acknowledge that existential migrations are almost always solitary, rather than mass migration or forced exodus. This solitude, and the associated lack of recognition from the settled majority, is not only quite poignant, but probably influences the lonely longing for specific homey interactions.

---

44. Rapport, 2003:119

CHAPTER 10
A PHILOSOPHY OF DWELLING AND HOMECOMING

What's so *existential* about existential migration? American philosopher Glen Gray suggests that the *mood* of existentialism could be described as 'a feeling of the homelessness of man'. The world we are thrown into cannot meet the claims of the human spirit. 'Our natural and social environment oppresses us with its foreignness, its unsuitability as a home for all that is specifically human about us as individuals'[45]. According to Gray, if we are sensitive to the human condition, we will not find a refuge in nature or society, we will remain outcasts. The existentialist's deep-rooted homelessness sets him or her apart from the idealist goal of finding one's home in oneself, society, or the ecologist's emphasis on the coziness of nature. However, the existentialists do not express a 'cynical hopelessness', but instead seek to balance *lack* with comradeship among the few like-minded individuals they encounter.

Following the German existentialist Martin Heidegger, Gray presents an evocative description of the existentialist's state of being which is almost indistinguishable from profound accounts of existential migration,

---

45. Gray, 1951: 114

> When you feel [not-at-home]… you are seized with a nameless fear. You are out of your element, but more than that you have an intuition of abysses hidden from normal moods. These rare experiences of the uncanny… are revelatory of the innermost nature of reality. At such times we feel a deep sense of unease; we are threatened and oppressed by everything in general and nothing in particular. We are filled with dread or anguish, a psychological state which has for the existentialists metaphysical origins… what has oppressed us is the primary intuition that we are not sustained by infinite power and plenitude of being… On the contrary, we, human creatures, perceive dimly in the experience of the uncanny, that the world rests on nothing. It has no basis or ground[46].

From this quote it is clear that the 'mood' of the existentialist has more than a little convergence with the affective experiences of many of the participants. The participants, nearly without exception, seem to have perceived *something* of the radical groundlessness of human existence and perhaps subsequently have not been capable of reconvincing themselves of the solidity of conventional forms of life. From an early age, some individuals have realized that they are fundamentally autonomous, cut adrift without an omnipotent parent or secure anchor against the fortuity of life. However, such sensitivities are uncommon. 'We are chiefly creatures of comfort, not seekers of truth'.[47] Yet the existential migrants interviewed explicitly stated their disdain for comfort, saying they need to sustain life by seeking unfamiliar and challenging situations in order to 'kick myself alive'. We see in existential migration a dread of the everyday intertwined with a motivated search. As Jaspers puts it, 'The bottomless character of the world must become revealed to us, if we are to win through to the truth of the world'[48].

The existential perspective attempts to view existence as it is, exposing distractions and evasions in order to acknowledge our freedom, limits, and fragility. This is the opposite of our primary desire for security, safety, protection, or the illusory containment of 'home'. The interviews

---

46. Ibid: 116
47. Gray, 1951: 117
48. Jaspers, 1932, Philosophie: 469, c.f. Gray, 1951:117

reveal the paradox of desiring 'home' in the sense of warm belonging, while embodying a broken-hearted insight that such comfort is deceptive and never convincing enough to camouflage insight. Instead, existing on the boundaries of life, with all the associated distress, offers at least the consolation of more immediate contact with the feeling of 'reality'. Such a way of being is not embarked upon once and for all; it requires constant choice, constant wariness of comforting self-deceptions. Of course the ultimate limit situation is death, and as we all die alone, perhaps some recognition of this generates the greater individualism of the 'existential migrant', the solitary character of the world-wanderer.

Sonia Kruks in her *Situation and Human Existence* points out that there is an overwhelming though misguided temptation for us to 'treat our own lives and those of our fellows as problems rather than as mysteries'. We cannot choose the circumstances we are born into, social class, language, location, etc. but as a conscious being, we must *choose our way of responding* to all those givens. I may be born into a working class family, but to be a worker requires my choice. This distinction sheds some possible light on the disjuncture between the participants and their home environments. Somehow it is as if they *could not choose* the most obvious givens offered by their traditions, conventions, and environmental expectations ('I *had to* go').

We often perceive ourselves to be more limited by situations than we are in fact. No action is *totally* free from the constraints of the situation it occurs in, yet it is never totally determined and constrained by the situation. This raises a question regarding a possible difference between existential migrants, who are intent upon expressing their freedom, and others who are unaware that choice even exists for them[49]. Being marginal, distant from the solid centre, helps to create a broader perspective on the situation and therefore awareness of

---

49. Yet at the same time, the participants also seem limit-bound and un-free in their inability to stay!

possibilities and choice. Such awareness of the freedom in man has been described as a 'hollow in Being', 'a place of unrest'[50].

Martin Heidegger's perspective emphasizes that each person is 'thrown' into existence, into a particular nation and culture at a particular point in its history, into a life that is already open to certain possibilities more than others. One's upbringing may make a particular kind of development and particular choices almost compulsory while others are next to impossible. The quandary seems to be that to respond 'authentically', a person must move beyond the given, further than one's inherited tradition. Existential migrants may exhibit an 'authentic' response in that they seek the *beyond*, exceeding the given culture through elaborations with unfamiliar traditions.

10.1 HOMEWORLD AND ALIENWORLD

In *Home and Beyond*, the philosopher Anthony Steinbock asks basic questions about what it actually means *to belong*, either to a family, a social group, or to an organization such that we can use the plural pronoun 'we' or possessive pronoun 'our'. Answers to such questions necessarily incorporate the problems of identity, difference, and who is to be considered an outsider or stranger. Steinbock's own contribution is to develop an approach that defines 'homeworlds' and 'alienworlds' as generating each other's existence. Steinbock asserts that the homeworld is not the original home world, the primary or most basic, but rather the one with a unique value.

According to Steinbock, the earth is home in a sense in which no other 'place' could be. The earth grounds everything, including the lifeworld, which is our historical and cultural territory, bordered and distinct as *homeworld* but necessitating the simultaneous creation of the outside *alienworld*. Steinbock says we constitute our homeworld

---

50. Merleau-Ponty, *Sense and Nonsense*, 1964: 65-6

by making the unknown familiar, emphasizing the sameness of things, making everything as we expect it to be. This is the process of reduction of the unheimlich, reducing arbitrary world to necessary earth in its hominess and comfort.

Steinboch says that when we "change places", move or migrate, 'we do not simply leave the terrain behind'[51]. By 'terrain' he means our familiar milieu and he reinforces his point with the slogan *'the terrain attaches to the lived-body'*. Homeworlds may make us happy or miserable, but regardless, they are privileged as *the* world from which we accrue our bodily comportment, our way of sensing, to the extent that Steinbock considers the lived-body as the "home-body". Steinbock clarifies his view by stating '… simply being in a particular location for some time and *having been born there* does not necessarily make a territory a homeworld' (*italics added*). A new house, for example, may not be home for a long time or it may never acquire the 'generative density of a sedimented tradition' and never 'draw me home …'. To reiterate, Steinbock proclaims that a homeworld is usually tied to a geographical location, like our birthplace, but the homeworld cannot be equated simply to our place of birth for this would restrict home simply to origin. A later childhood residence may be more home than the first one. Even a nomad has a homeworld, and a homeworld can exist in the future as in 'the promised land'. Of course the participants have made explicit that *having* a homeworld and *feeling* at-home need to be distinguished.

Constructing a familiar home area simultaneously demarcates another world, where our conceptual systems do not work, an 'abnormal' world where our own assumptions and values are alien. Steinbock perceives that the familiar world is constituted by what is taken for granted by a person. Steinbock continues by saying that the ability to make something typical 'is the essential means of human normality to ensure against the existential shock of having to see the world the way

---

51. This section refers to Steinbock, 1995: 166- 240.

it is.' However, does all typifying necessarily consist of reducing the unfamiliar and alien to sameness?

According to Steinbock, the perspective of home as normal lifeworld generates the experience of the alienworld *as not normal, nor home for me*. He is inferring that the alien is 'other' and the home is known, so our relations to each will incorporate these qualitative distinctions. However, through the participant interviews we've seen that one can also feel 'alien' at home, and finding one's home an alien place is not the same as finding an alien place alien (as our interviewees corroborate). Likewise feeling at home in an alienworld is not the same as finding an experience of home in one's homeworld. The ability to feel at-home in the alien does not eradicate the unique significance of the homeworld, but the perspective of home and alien need not be normal and abnormal in the simple manner he has outlined.

The interviews illustrate that it's not valid to equate 'homeworld' with the sense of a shared belonging. This is not to deny that the homeworld is uniquely significant in *some* way, leaving an imprint that enables us to discriminate between the original, the home, and the alien lifeworlds. Our comparisons between worlds are not arbitrary. Alienness requires comparison to a homeworld as distinct from any other lifeworld, but the felt quality of that comparison may vary greatly from the conventional modes being presented by Steinbock. We can adopt various responses to our homeworld, for example, critical or apologetic stances, but both of these can still be based in belonging – presumably a person can feel profound belonging to a home culture of which they are also critical (think of the many Americans critical of their home country under the Bush regime). But it is a different matter to adopt various responses, critique, resistance, subservience, or flight, towards a homeworld where one has had little sense of belonging. For a person to be able to contemplate 'escape' he or she must have developed some degree of a 'critical attitude', a perspective that allows assessment of pre-given cultural convictions. This allows the *possibility* of being freed from naïvely and complacently swallowing a tradition whole.

We need to re-think many taken for granted concepts in order to account for the experiences of existential migration. We need to ask, what does it actually mean to not-belong to the coherent given world we are thrown into? For example, if leaving signifies releasement from the tight hold of the homeworld, does it simultaneously constitute the homeworld letting go of us; not-belonging may be a two-way process even if its recognition is more obvious in the one leaving. It insinuates that the traditional homeworld would rather maintain its cultural solidity than modify itself enough to accept the full diversity of its own membership.

Steinbock introduces the term 'homecomrade' to refer to those others who feel familiar to me, who I feel most at-home with, with whom I share important rituals and customs. He or she 'bears' the same world that I do. Typically it is assumed that homecomrades share one's original home *place* and its sameness, but the term presents an interesting possibility. Although existential migrants have cultural traditions they share with their homeworld, it can be asked, who *really* is the 'homecomrade' of an existential migrant? Based upon the participant stories, I would propose that a homecomrade for us is more likely to be another person engaged in existential migration rather than an individual who shares the home rituals and customs. In fact for some of our participants, exemplified in Patricia's transcript, meeting someone from 'home' is an experience that accentuates alienness rather than familiarity or comradeship.

Individuals engaged in existential migration seem to 'recognize' each other enough to congregate together; some participants even referring to a 'tribe', a wandering lost tribe. If it is reasonable to suggest that existential migration generates temporary groups of 'homecomrades' we are on the brink of proposing the existence of 'an alternative human history', one based upon solitary migrations as opposed to the edifices of settled collective history, and one that has not been acknowledged or recorded as such. This interpretation of homecomrade can be read into Steinbock's view,

> We may recognize another homecomrade on this basis of this or that familiarity. Familiarity can show itself through a particular style of dress, typical smells of food, typically familiar accents. We may recognize a homecomrade... by the way they cross the street when the light is red... by the values they hold etc[52].

The above ideas foster the following new refinements.

1. There is an apparent bias towards the sedentary in philosophy, despite token acknowledgement of migratory experiences. Both homeworld and homecomrade are for the most part geographically based concepts. Steinbock offers no scope for the homeworld to be constituted in otherness rather than sameness – according to this account one cannot be most at-home in the foreign or the unheimlich.
2. Steinbock assumes that the transformation of the unknown to the familiar results in hominess and reduction of the unheimlich, yet the participants also certainly *knew* their worlds without that familiarity obscuring their unheimlich awareness of not belonging.
3. We acquire our bodily comportment, the way we move, talk, make gestures, facial expressions, in a homeworld culture, even if we reject that culture. Even a native North American critical of his own culture and living in London has a form of North American deportment but perhaps not a typical one. His critical not-belonging to the homeworld is also presumably part of this implicit behaviour – we don't just accrue a heritage without simultaneously incorporating our values towards that inheritance. He may seem somewhat less American to others, especially other Americans, but still somehow recognizably American.

---

52. Steinbock, 1995: 224

4. Existential migrants may comprise a permeable and intangible *alternative human history* yet to be chronicled in any substantive way.

10.2 WORLD ALIENATION AND THE UNHEIMLICH

Steinbock's analysis causes him to lament the contemporary efforts to create a world *sans frontiers*. He sees it as an attempt to make home and alien interchangeable and believes such attempts mistakenly assume home and alien are symmetrically accessible, that we can achieve a kind of amorphous internationalism. Likewise, Peter Read says ignoring the importance of home-place in the modern world results in 'creeping international sameness', a 'tabula rasa' which aspires to a condition of 'absolute placelessness'. The following sections address contemporary modes of living that are developing within creeping internationalism and the ramifications of all this. These discussions take a different path than that taken by Steinbock and Read.

Modern tourism studies extend far beyond what we usually consider to be conventional tourism *per se*, utilizing the topic to investigate the 'modern consciousness' and our contemporary worldview in general. Some tourist researchers are shifting the focus from tourist sights to the experience of the individual tourist in order to concentrate upon the *personal or intersubjective feelings* aroused by travel. As a reaction to the triumph of pretence over sincerity in modern life, some tourists are beginning to resist passive consumerism in order to become creatively engaged in travel.

> People are nostalgic ... they want to re-live [more authentic ways of being] in the form of tourism at least temporally, empathically, and symbolically... Tourism is thus regarded as a simpler, freer, more spontaneous, more authentic, or less serious, less utilitarian, and romantic, lifestyle which enables people to keep a distance from, or transcend, daily lives[53].

---

53. Wang, 1999:358

These values, including dissatisfaction with mundane everyday life, harmonize with the descriptions of many existential migrants, and I would guess that 'existential tourism' could be considered a sporadic expression of, or occasionally the initiation of, a process of 'existential migration'. In both processes, adventure becomes a counterbalance and compensation for boredom, lack of authentic novelty, and loss of meaning. However, these brief touristic interludes are not the same as more long-standing and integral ways of being as described by the participants. For example, does an annual 'authentic tourist experience' challenge or facilitate ongoing adaptation to unsatisfying forms of life for the rest of the year? It is unclear whether these tourist studies have mistakenly taken a snapshot of the on-going process of existential migration, or if they describe another process altogether. We have much still to understand about emerging responses to living in the 21st century global flux.

Recent developments in Japanese touristic experiences reinvigorate the image of the disenchanted and alienated young western traveller who seeks meaning in culturally diverse alternatives. One researcher perceives this recurrence as a form of what he terms 'therapeutic tourism', exemplified in the college student studying abroad, the graduate taking time off to travel, and the ecotourist's escape from city life. These journeys entail an intense personal commitment, a lived process that is different in quality to the typical package holiday. The stories of existential migration often describe the use of such travel experiences as the commencement of leaving home, sampling a taste of the possible life 'out there'[54].

The research cited above analyzes the recent shift in Japanese tourism as a comment upon lost potentialities in the Japanese homeland.

---

54. From Rea, 2000. Singh (2002) also points out that tourism can lead to permanent migration and tourists on this trajectory are generally classified as 'wanderlusts, drifters, existentials [sic]'(Ibid:262) and have much in common with many anthropologists who end up settling down in a society that was originally the object of study. Singh believes that this phenomenon requires study. Hopefully the current research is a preliminary response to his suggestion.

This innovative tourism manifests as almost pilgrim-like journeys to foreign sites, which function as traditional Japanese *furusatos*, and are even marketed as such. The *furusato* used to be found domestically, in remote countryside locations, offering a 'traditional, pre-modern home' of rustic simplicity and spiritual centeredness. The fact that *furusatos* are now sought outside Japan is seen as the consequence of a state of homelessness in Japanese society linked to social shocks in the early 1990s, combined with an associated new willingness 'to seek existential meaning outside of Japan'[55]. Seen through the conceptualization of home as interaction, it might be envisaged that for some Japanese citizens Japan no longer engenders the interaction that allows them to say 'I feel at home, I belong' whereas these foreign unfamiliar places with which they 'wholeheartedly identify' actually allow a temporary interaction of 'home' though they are ostensibly foreign through and through. Somehow, for *some* Japanese individuals, these places generate a 'matching', that is deeply felt. This development does not appear surprising to us in that it evokes reminiscence of the experiences of many participants who felt more at home in totally foreign places. Based upon interviews with Japanese tourists at various foreign furusato sites, the researchers echo aspects of the emerging understanding of existential migration,

> What has been proposed is that to a new generation Japan is not the home it was to their parents and that it often fails as a source of either modern or traditional comfort. For a growing number, succour has been found in the tradition of the West, and young Japanese are fulfilling dreams by actually going to them, where they feel light and free and at home… Happier abroad, they express their distaste for the rigid social mores of home… many Japanese … [in their search for authenticity, are] going out into the great big world, *less and less in tour groups*, and are immersing themselves in the fields and woods and hospitality of places thought still pristine…[56].

This last italicized comment addresses a potential divergence between the two concepts, i.e. that 'existential migration' does not constitute

---

55. Rea, 2000: 643
56. Rea, 2000: 658, *italics added*

an identifiable social experience, nor is it typified by group arrivals on pre-arranged tour buses. Another dissimilarity appears to be that the furusato experience is one of nostalgia mostly for a national past rather than based upon attraction to different foreign cultures encountered in the present. The furusato seems to consist in a retreat from the homelessness of modernity merged with a profound quest for something more Japanese, or more *heimlich*, than Japan can currently offer.

In contrast to the quest to revive lost connection as described above, the travel writer Pico Iyer profiles journeys through our increasingly diffuse and borderless world. In *The Global Soul – Jet-lag, shopping malls, and the search for home*, Iyer suggests a new kind of being may be emerging: a multi-cultural fusion, a cross-border confusion, a hodgepodge itinerant with a porous sense of self, and he depicts this world homelessness in the concept of 'global soul'. According to Iyer, one country or one fixed community is no longer enough, so the global soul, if he or she has *any* sense of home, has only the 'home' that emanates from 'the ties and talismans he carries around with him'. Iyer argues that previously our notions of home, past, and community were givens, often oppressively so, however now it is possible to *select* even the most fundamental details of one's life. Despite this strange *a la carte* self, Iyer also periodically recognizes the enduring call of something called 'home'. An Indian cabbie living in Toronto expresses it this way; 'Where you spent your childhood, sir, you can never forget that place. I am here, sir, and I like it here. But' – and I could hear the ache – 'I love my India'[57].

Iyer grew up in three different cultures. He differentiates himself from an exile (who looks back at a home he once had), an expatriate (posted abroad to make a living), a nomad (wanders according to traditional or seasonal patterns), a refugee (violently forced to migrate): He is a 'global soul', a person who falls between these categories and yet does

---

57. Iyer,2000:22

not fit into any settled community. Iyer writes of the positive facets of his position in the world, everywhere is new and strange, keeping alive a sense of wonder and detachment. He feels enabled to 'live a little bit above parochialisms', able to see places with a 'flexible eye'; he says 'the very notion of home is foreign to me, as the state of foreignness is the closest thing I know to home'. The last chapter of Iyer's text is entitled 'The Alien Home' and opens with the conclusion that the only home a global soul can find in today's world is 'in the midst of the alien and the indecipherable'. Of himself, Iyer proclaims he is,

> ... a wanderer from birth, like more and more around me, I choose to live a long way from the place where I was born, the country in which I work, and the land to which my face and blood assign me – on a distant island where I can't read any of the signs and will never be accepted as even a partial native[58].

Iyer admits that Japan, where he lives, will never be his home, except in a superficial way. In return, Japan would not want him to presume to claim otherwise. There is a mutually agreed convivial distance that seems to suit him. A global soul, a citizen of nowhere, could, of course, be perceived as a threat to settled civic harmony.

Iyer's 'global soul' appears to acquiesce to the homelessness experienced by some in the modern world and as such lacks the heartfelt conciliatory quest of the existential tourist. In his text, Iyer articulates values also associated with processes of existential migration; attributes which differ considerably from the settled population. However, he accentuates positive and desired attributes of these experiences while neglecting the more troublesome feelings of loss and the impetus for continued quests for 'home' however hopeless. He proclaims that the notion of home is foreign to him yet goes on to say that his state of foreignness is his approximation of home. Lacking an actual *place* he can call home is not the same as saying one lacks the ability to experience 'at-homeness' at all; conversely, foreignness may be Iyer's

---

58. Iyer, 2000: 269

'home' yet not provide an *experience* of being at-home. Like Iyer, the existential migrants also celebrate the positive reverberations of leaving home, but unlike Iyer, they don't neglect the heartfelt yearning and continued sense of loss that colours homelessness. Iyer hypothesizes that *the questions* raised by modernity may be our home now: we might find we can live in the 'uncertainties' we carry around with us. Again, rather than evaporate, the issue of locating home seems to haunt Iyer –can one really dwell in a question? What would such dwelling feel like? The philosophy of Martin Heidegger seems to offer possibilities for clarifying and carrying forward a more philosophical discourse on these issues. Let's look a bit more at Heidegger's perspective, though still only briefly.

For Heidegger, the 'unheimlich'[59] feeling reveals that we each drift along without any firm ground, forever *cadavering* towards our own demise. The certainty we feel in daily life camouflages the uncanniness of human existence: we tranquillize ourselves with details. However, rumbling along underneath this taken-for-granted certainty is an anxiety (or angst) regarding our insecurity, suddenly revealing itself in otherwise harmless situations. When anxiety surfaces, it is something like an 'alien' call' to recover ourselves from our submersion in the everyday. This call constitutes an opportunity to the everyday individual to heed his or her potential to be more fully alive. This is a call that has no content, it does not tell us what to do, and it offers no guiding message other than to expose the illusion of a cozy secure world.

Angst recovers us from being lost in details. We comprehend that the world cannot offer the secure home it appears to offer and in response we experience the 'unheimlich', a kind of homesickness for a secure world that never was. It temporarily discloses to us the brute fact *that we exist without any guarantees*. To respond to this call we must stand apart from the mass of 'normal living'. It is a strange inversion of lost

---

59. I will use these terms unheimlich and uncanny quite interchangeably as both terms are used by different authors to translate a similar experience.

and found in which we *find* ourselves most fully at the moment when the world sinks into insignificance and we appear most *lost* in the eyes of the conventional.

Heidegger's analysis touches upon facets of the experiences of existential or therapeutic tourism, 'global soul', and existential migration. It inverts our usual understandings of identity and motivation, offers different experiences of belonging, and suggests deeper meanings of home. Heidegger's ideas seem to set the stage for a celebration of the existential migrant as 'existential hero'. True, these individuals consistently disparage the conventionally unaware lives they encountered at home, opting instead to unsettle themselves through confrontation with foreignness. Many of the participants also reported feeling anxious, living in a kind of restlessness that may illustrate at least a momentary attuning with the unheimlich homelessness of Heidegger's authentic being. The importance of choice, independence, solitude, and freedom, evident in the participant stories, clearly do not convey collusion with tranquillizing 'normality'.

This book must raise more questions than it answers, as the concept of existential migration is very new. Notwithstanding this disclaimer, from the current vantage point, it seems that existential migration constitutes *both* an awareness of our groundlessness, and a fleeing from confrontation with the givens that are revealed when habit breaks down. Experiencing our primordial homelessness is presumably disconcerting, so it is not surprising that we inevitably 'fall' back into the mundane and anaesthetizing world. The fact that our participants seem to continue to look for 'home' in some form, indicates that at least in some moments, they seek the tranquillized 'at-homeness' that they are nonetheless unconvinced by. Being-at-home may be the most effective and enduring camouflage for our existential unsettledness, however, once exposed as such, the façade of home may never regain its previous potency to obscure and reassure. It is *as if* at some point something in the individual opens to 'the unknown', instigating for some a process of existential migration. Presumably not all such 'openings' lead to this process of leaving home but I would suggest that to some extent the stories of migration in this book imply this openness to sensing the unheimlich. Angst may motivate the flight, the need to escape, pushing individuals continuously on to new adventures, one step ahead of realizations that are difficult to bear or to incorporate into a lived biography. But this is speculation. And *if* our primary nature is to be anxiously not-at-home, and recognition of this in turn instigates the desire to settle at home, which then gives rise to yet another call to authenticity, then we are in a perpetual cycle and in what sense can we actually *be* on earth at all? Yet we are.

This chapter sorties into the philosophical and as such begins to speculate away from the experiences of the participants, for example:

1. Unlike 'existential tourism' or the 'global soul', the new concept of 'existential migration' embodies the whole spectrum of difficult and positive aspects of 'homelessness', both displacement and the insatiable yearning for home, without prioritizing or pathologizing either. This seems unique in that most commentators align themselves with either the 'positive' or 'negative' aspects of these experiences.
2. The authentic 'call of conscience' is individual and requires some separation from 'the mass'. Perhaps this sheds light on the individualistic nature of existential migration – it has a strong tendency to manifest as solitary leaving.
3. The motivation for existential migration may be similar to Heidegger's 'universal call', issuing from no one in particular, with no distinct guiding message – similar in nature to each participant's report 'I *had to* go' out into the world, without a clear direction and usually no clear goal.
4. The concept of existential migration is future-oriented, not just tied to the past as in nostalgia.

10.3 DWELLING AND HOMECOMING

In his book *Building, Dwelling, Thinking*[60], Heidegger says that we must *learn* to dwell within our existence; it is not automatic. As a species we have forgotten that our main plight in life is the question of how to dwell, to live in our uniquely human way. Heidegger believes that contemplating our homelessness in the world 'is the sole summons that *calls* mortals into their dwelling'. The first great obstacle to understanding ourselves is our tendency to ignore what deserves to be questioned because it seems so obvious. Here then is a paradox: the strangeness of the not-at-home offers us an 'authentic dwelling place', a 'home' qualitatively different from an inauthentic taken-for-granted hominess.

Heidegger's thought recalls the plight of existential migration, in which some individuals have made the difficult solitary choice to pursue their potential, often leaving uncomprehending family and friends behind. Herein we configure a homelessness that calls us to 'authentic dwelling' where we preserve the essence of what is human. We dwell most honestly in the awareness of how strange our existence really is. Without this homelessness we do not dwell. Existential migration is an invitation to dwelling, an invitation requiring choice.

10.3.1 Homecoming and the Return Home

Even those individuals who choose to leave home continue to live in some relation to the question of return. Some want to return, or are vexed by the question of whether it is possible, while others say they would never return, but no one was indifferent to the issue. Feelings about returning home seem to change depending on circumstances at home or in the foreign place, with perhaps some indication that feelings of wanting to return increase as people age. Returning home to settle can be a complex geo-psychological task and an opportunity to assess the transformations that have occurred

---

60. This section taken from comments in Heidegger, 1964: 347-63

in one's self while away. For some people this return is a psychological and philosophical process of healing as much as a geographical process of relocation. The difficulties of return increase the longer one remains away; over time the individual and the homeland respectively continue to evolve, moving further apart.

It is often assumed that the return home or the contemplated return is instigated by feelings of 'homesickness'. It is noteworthy that 'homesickness' as a term was rarely mentioned in the interviews and did not emerge as a distinct theme. However, one would think that it features somehow in the complex feelings about returning home, so it seems appropriate to briefly explore it here. In an article on the history of nostalgia, Stephanie Pain describes the 'terrible longing for home' experienced by Swiss soldiers serving as mercenaries[61]. It refers to medical observations made in the late 17th century that some of the soldiers wanted to go home so badly that if they couldn't return they died. The diagnosis was termed 'nostalgia' and it had a list of associated symptoms and prescribed treatments. The potentially fatal disease was also observed amongst foreign students and in one account the student suffering from 'homesickness' or nostalgia, began to improve immediately upon the suggestion that he or she could return home. Johannes Hofer, the young medical student who coined the term 'nostalgia' concluded that it especially afflicted 'those *forced* to leave home and who found it hard to adjust to strange people and customs'[62]. First signs of the disease were detected when the victim wandered about sad, scorned foreign manners, couldn't sleep and thought only of their homeland. Though there were a variety of disgusting 'treatments', the main remedy was to give the patient all hope that they could return home when physically well enough. The diagnosis spread and became established as medical fact, confirmed by a post mortem revealing changes in the brain, heart, lungs, and intestines. The syndrome passed from fashion but was temporarily revived during

---

61. Pain, 2003.
62. Pain, 2003:48.

the American civil war, when Union soldiers fighting far from home displayed the same symptoms, with 58 soldiers eventually dying from 'nostalgia'. Eventually psychiatrists introduced new syndromes; depression, nervous breakdown, anorexia, and malingering, and 'nostalgia' as a medical diagnosis was consigned to history.

In her exploration of the topic, Anne Winning writes that homesickness indicates the missing of a place where we feel a sense of 'ownness' or intimate familiarity. In saying this, she once again equates the familiar with safety, a sense of belonging and intimate connection. While this may often be the case, we know that an experience of the familiar is not the only experience that can be longed for, even desperately. Some people apparently suffer from 'far-sickness', a kind of 'homesickness' for the strange, the unknown, and the foreign. We need a broader definition of 'home'-sickness than that based upon a conventional prioritizing of sedentary sameness. From our participants we learn that we can long for home without any intention of ever returning home, in essence homesick for something lost but not necessarily for something that can be retrieved from the cozy and familiar home culture. In existential migration a person may leave home yet never shake its haunting presence, long for home yet undoubtedly see no future for him or herself there. Paradoxically, we have maintained a 'special connection' to a homeworld even though we may rarely have *felt at-home* there. It may be this quandary that contributes such poignancy to the dilemmas of leaving or staying, returning or wandering on.

The return home highlights the significance of being excluded from all the intervening living that can never be regained. 'I am ... part of and not part of, part of but not belonging'[63]. Though the one who left home remains part of the family, he or she is now an outsider, the gap they left having been filled in long ago so that they are no longer necessary in those deep-seated family interactions. There is a sense

---

63. Shaw, 2002:4

that one should belong but that one no longer does; the returnee's role is artificial in the pathways of everyday family life. *The one who left, can, at best, be special.* We have elaborated ourselves within numerous new settings. Likewise, the ones who stayed have also continued to live, so that when we return, body-to-body again, there is a collision of the intervening years. The dynamic of staying, leaving, and returning, can be inscribed into the definition of home,

> The symbolic character of the notion "home" is emotionally evocative and hard to describe ... home means one thing to the man who has never left it, another thing to the man who lives far from it, and still another to him who returns ... [it] is an expression of the highest degree of familiarity and intimacy[64].

Man sets out towards that which is different and always returns to the 'same', yet, not 'same' as in identical because he who returns has in the interim been changed by time, voyage, adventure, longing… In Andrzej Warminski's reading of Heidegger, it is clear that man is more unheimlich than anything else unheimlich because man's essence is in 'coming to be at home' which means man's essence is in *coming*, not *'being'* at home'. If 'man has to *come to be* at home, then he *is* not at home; if man *is* not at home, then he has to *come to be* at home'[65]. Of course this 'coming to be at home' implies that man is perhaps always not-at-home.

This brings us to one of the most important statements we can make from this new research: Existential migration suggests that we are not-at-home *not* because we have been exiled from home, but rather because we have been *exiled by home from ourselves*. The tranquillizing home distances us from the incomplete self that calls to be known. This call is silenced in the mass, which remain safe and secure, comfortable and lost, *at home*. The coming-to-be-at-home in the foreign is perhaps a *being found*, found in an authentic relation with the unheimlich

---

64. Schutz, 1971:107-108, c.f. Shaw, 2002:7
65. Warminski, 1990: 199

dimension of human life – coming home to homelessness though never *being at home*.

Heidegger continued to be preoccupied with the question of home during his life. His later thought epitomizes the entire human situation as one of deep homelessness, 'meaning that on this earth we have no abiding home, since we are not embedded in the world as a part of nature. Instead we are, as it were, thrown into the world, into a life we did not choose but which, now we are here, we must choose or, in one of myriad ways, evade'[66]. For example, giving a lecture in his hometown in 1961, Heidegger refers to the television aerials atop most roofs as signifying a future where most of us will no longer be 'at home' even in our own homes. The television tempts me to be somewhere else, on safari, at the match, in the midst of another family's drama. Heidegger is concerned that the whole of humanity is forgetting itself and sailing into a forsaken state of lostness. This is not the authentic unheimlich but rather an alienated disorientation. Heidegger says that those who wander far from home, in remote places, are capable of bringing back the message concerning the origins that have otherwise been forgotten. This origin can only be pointed at poetically. *According to Heidegger, what is most authentic for humanity is always what is out of the ordinary.* Such sentiments clearly echo the attitudes and experiences of many of the participants.

Homecoming, then, is not the return home to a geographical place, but more a *return* from our superficial commercial hominess back into the mystery of the world. These ideas have obvious relevance to the increasing globalization and market-dominated forms of living in the 21st century. We are in danger of entering an era of lostness, the end of belonging in either its restricted conforming sense or its open authentic sense. It is disturbing to witness the reactive backlash that is growing against this global lostness. In reaction to feeling lost we

---

66. Warminski, 1990: 199. As in Graciella's comment, 'this is where I was put to grow up'.

have seen recent attempts to assert the most vicious manifestation of 'home' by forceful imposition: for example the rise of nationalism, tribalism, religious fundamentalism, these are all complex phenomena but on some level they are efforts to reduce the world to the security of sameness.

In a series of lecture courses in Freiburg in the middle of World War Two, Heidegger said that 'confrontation with otherness and the alien' allows a kind of self-discovery of one's endowments. The self goes abroad not to 'get lost in strangeness' but to 'ready itself there for its own tasks'. Patient and sustained reflection is required. Self-discovery points to a 'homecoming', a return home to the truths of human existence. This is not adventure for adventure's sake, it is not a self-indulgent addiction to excitement, rather it is a subdued and reticent 'reflective glimpse' of oneself. It is important to understand that 'adventure' in the sense criticized here, is a kind of macho, hard-nosed conquering attitude toward otherness and a way of avoiding the mysterious world awaiting discovery[67]. Heidegger is extolling a transformative 'hero's journey' as an autodidactic process in which the journey abroad is also a return to the self as the only site of possible transformation.

Homecoming has no fixed abode, but rather it indicates an 'in-between place of transit – a zone located between self and other, between proximity and distance, and also between mortals and immortals'[68]. *Humans are unique in our sense of alienation and alone in our need for homecoming.* Rather than an adventurer, an itinerant wandering from place to place driven by curiosity, we are driven to diligently traverse the earth's terrain looking to come home. The adventurer in contrast, is a spurious figure not interested in learning, intent on denying home,

---

67. Such 'adventure' is scarcely deserving of the term as its motive is to appropriate the unknown into unreflective hominess even when abroad. It really is the opposite of adventure in the existential sense, a retreat from the real adventure of confronting the mysteries of existence.
68. Dallmayr,1993:159

attempting to indiscriminately substitute the arbitrarily foreign for home, and 'thereby losing the sense of either place'[69].

Dwelling does not refer to possessing accommodation. Dwelling grounds human essence - it is an experiential setting down of the human on earth. Accordingly, the spiritual and mystical spheres deepen the migratory process.

10.3.2 Homecoming as a Spiritual Belonging

Leaving can initiate a spiritual quest that was stifled at home. Travel is a mode of 'conscious living', keeping a person aware of surroundings and preventing a slip into habitual and less mindful ways of being. Exploring the world can be guided by an intuitive connection to a transpersonal dimension. Seeking out contact with strange cultures offers the experience of 'mystery' in the world, opening the self to one's own mysterious being. The connection between personal and global mystery can generate a temporary feeling of belonging in the universe. The return home, after years abroad, can generate a spiritual dimension of reconnection and psychological healing.

Moments of communion in which the self-world boundary seems to dissolve, offer departure points into deeper spiritual development. The implication is that this experience is intrinsic to all human beings though we have all sorts of ways of erecting defensive barriers against it.

In a unique and moving text, *Eternal Echoes - Exploring our Hunger to Belong*, the Irish writer John O'Donohue presents 'belonging' as the human attempt to bridge the gap between isolation and intimacy. It is, he thinks, far more important than status, achievement and possessions, and without a true sense of belonging, life is empty and pointless. At the heart of individuality there is a profound necessity, a hunger to belong,

---

69. Dallmayr, 1993: 163

> To be human is to belong. Belonging is a circle that embraces everything; if we reject it, we damage our nature. The word 'belonging' holds together two fundamental aspects of life: being and longing, the Longing of our being and the Being of our longing. Belonging is deep; only in a superficial sense does it refer to our external attachment to people, places and things ... Our life's journey is the task of refining our belonging so that it may become more true, loving, good and free. We do not have to force belonging. The longing within us always draws us towards belonging, and again towards new forms of belonging, when we have outgrown the old ones[70].

Clearly, O'Donohue is not advocating a mode of belonging which is simply a flight from deep realities, 'When you suppress your wild longing and opt for the predictable and safe forms of belonging, you sin against the rest of nature that longs to live deeply through you'. There is a 'voice of longing' awakening the knowledge that something unnameable is missing, forcing some individuals to 'begin a haunted journey on a never-ending path in quest of the something that is missing...' O'Donohue, reminiscent of Heidegger and compatible with some of the participant interviews, suggests that we are 'relentless pilgrims' on earth and that our unease is natural and inconsolable. The belonging of the pilgrim and the native differs, and the wanderer's presence is easily identified and made marginal. According to O'Donohue, this wanderer prioritizes longing over belonging. No place can convincingly lay claim to the wanderer. 'A new horizon always calls'. O'Dononue, consistent with themes of existential migration, cannot answer why such a person is committed to foreign adventure, values freedom, and travels with an urgency that has no goal. To him or her, staying in one place is more a threat than any change could be. In his evocative descriptions, O'Donohue closely approximates the questions and elaborations of existential migration though in considerably more poetic and romantic language.

> The soul and the spirit are wanderers; their place of origin and destination remain unknown; they are dedicated to the discovery of what is unknown and strange[71].

---

70. O'Donohue, 1998:3
71. Ibid: 68

Society is designed to quell the voice of lonesomeness and banishment within each of us, but thereby exiling an essential part of the human being. Domestication reduces our humanity and our 'authentic' attempts to come to terms with wilderness, both fertile and lonely, both psychic and environmental. This is a homecoming to the intimate mysteries of life that remain untamed and undomesticated. O'Donohue says, 'The homeless mind is haunted by a sense of absence that it can neither understand nor transfigure'. The lost tribe of existential migrants could be thought of as 'spiritual strays'.

10.3.3 The Mythic History of Coming Home

It is widely acknowledged[72] that world mythology takes the motif of migration and homecoming as one of its central themes. The myth of Genesis could be read as one story of humankind's first exile from home. Such seminal narratives illustrate tragic dilemmas, suggesting that *something* fundamental about the human condition is expressed in stories of leaving. There are various myths of exile in the Greek, Christian, Celtic and Judaic traditions. Homer's *Odyssey* distinguishes between simple 'return' and the deeper process of homecoming - a gradual re-connecting and reintegration with home, including new self-awareness. This raises the question of why there is no acknowledgement of existential migration in the contemporary world compared with the myriad examples of stories in ancient and classic literature? Below is an exception, a popular twentieth century example of the heartfelt experience of leaving and coming 'home'.

One interpretation of the final pages of *The Return of the King*, the ultimate book of Tolkien's trilogy, *The Lord of the Rings*, suggests themes of migration, the hero's journey, and exile. The story ends with the return of the main characters to their homeland in the Shire but the primary hero of the story, Frodo, has suffered an injury in the course of his mission to save the world from darkness. Tolkien describes the

---

72. See for example Joseph Campbell, 2004.

return to the Shire in sentiments which at once take on a metaphoric tone, evoking comparison with the stories of existential migration described by participants. For example, Frodo, in conversation with the wise wizard Gandalf, refers to the wound in his shoulder as they ride towards home. In response Gandalf says,

> 'Alas! There are some wounds that cannot be wholly cured'.
> 'I fear it may be so with mine', said Frodo. 'There is no real going back. Though I may come to the Shire, it will not seem the same; for I shall not be the same. I am wounded with knife, sting, and tooth, and a long burden. Where shall I find rest?'
> Gandalf did not answer[73].

As they near the Shire, one of Frodo's companions remarks on their entry back into familiar lands and how their adventures and former comrades from other lands are already fading from his memory as if it was all a dream, to which Frodo responds, 'Not to me', said Frodo. 'To me [returning home] feels more like falling asleep again'. There has always been something different about Frodo, for example his intense interest in the adventures of the wide world recounted by his eccentric uncle. Now, having experienced other lands for himself, and his subsequent loss of innocence, Frodo cannot adapt back to the genteel life of the Shire. Not that Frodo had lost his love of the place, no, that was as intact for him as it was for his companions. But unlike his companions, Frodo could not stay. Sam, his closest friend settles down and marries, the Shire is the only place he really wants to be, though he still feels a loyalty to follow his 'master' Frodo, and thus feels 'torn in two'. Frodo acknowledges this, 'Poor Sam! It will feel like that, I am afraid'... 'But you will be healed. You were meant to be solid and whole and you will be'. Sam does not understand Frodo's need to leave, 'I thought that you were going to enjoy the Shire, too, for years and years, after all you have done'. Frodo replies,

> 'I thought so too, once. But I have been too deeply hurt, Sam. I tried to save the Shire, and it has been saved, but not for me. It must often be so, Sam,

---

73. Tolkien, 1967: 323

when things are in danger: some one has to give them up, lose them, so that others may keep them...'[74].

Frodo rides off with Gandalf and Sam returns to his wife, children, and home, where the fire is lit and the evening meal prepared. The combination of powerful themes in Tolkien's opus lends it to inexhaustible various readings. I offer only that this section serves, among many other things, as an example of the loss and ambivalent desires of what I am calling existential migration, including the sorrow of leaving, return, and leaving behind. Frodo is not leaving for riches or to escape oppression. He is leaving because his 'wound', a consequence of *who he is*, interacts with his world in such a way that he can no longer be at home 'at home'. There is no settlement for Frodo, *and this is how it should be*. Only by stating it this strongly can we unsettle the depth of our bias in favour of home. In the next chapter I will describe how some of the evocative writing of migrant authors and their accounts of leaving home and being foreigners, adds some poetry to the concept of existential migration.

This chapter implies that what we learn from existential migrants may have broad significance for our understanding of human beings in general. Following are some issues highlighted by the discussion above:

1. The concept of existential migration offers new definitions for 'home', 'homelessness', 'belonging', 'homecoming', often polar opposite meanings to their more everyday uses.
2. We can distinguish between authentic homelessness and lostness. 'Authentic homelessness' offers the potential for human dwelling while remaining aware of the unheimlich dimension in existence. 'Lostness' signifies either a conventionally sedating 'hominess' or aimless wandering.
3. Existential migration emerges with psychological, philosophical

---

74. Tolkien, 1967: 376

and spiritual dimensions, however this process might also 'degrade' into distracting adventure.
4. The 'call' to leave home may manifest in similar ways to the 'call of conscience' in that participants have described 'having to go' but without destination or clear goal. If so, then the term *existential* migration seems validated and may constitute, for some individuals, a transitory remembrance of authentic being.
5. *The concept of existential migration clarifies the possibility that 'home' in its conventional sense constitutes* true *exile* from values such as authenticity, awareness, pursuing self-potential, freedom, and the ineffability of existence. One's *orienting values* determine which process is considered exile and which is 'home'.

CHAPTER 11
SENSITIVITIES IN EXISTENTIAL MIGRATION

Life is meaningless unless it is self-directed, and some degree of personal space is necessary for the kind of contemplation that allows free choice. Migration can offer escape from encroachment and protection for freedom and independence. To feel unfree is deeply distressing, approximating the death of one's individuality. To follow the path to independence, freedom and choice, one must trust one's own voice, and have a degree of confidence in that 'voice'. Unfamiliar situations offer the challenge of continuous development while the comfort of the familiar is felt as stagnation. It remains a mystery why these specific individuals exhibit these values, so at odds with the surrounding milieu. There may be sedentary expressions of the values evident in existential migration, for example the 'inner journeying' of personal growth/spiritualism, academic studies, and social activism.

The sensitivities of a person in a process of existential migration have already been explored in sections on identity, belonging, and home. Here they are reconsidered more closely. For example, there is a common distinction made between 'freedom from' and 'freedom to', also called 'reflective' and 'reactive' autonomy[75]. Reflective autonomy refers to having a sense of freedom and choice about one's actions,

---

75. Sato and McCann, 1998

and reactive autonomy refers to a tendency to function defensively and withdraw from social interactions in order to avoid the impinging influence of others. On the basis of the participant interviews, there is evidence of both types of autonomy – with indications that in order to have a sense of *free choice to* self-determination there must pre-exist some sense of *freedom from* the intrusive encroachment by others, and homogeneous culture generally. Perhaps in a claustrophobic home environment one can attempt a protective withdrawal into isolated self-reflection, but this suggests a poor approximation of the autonomy offered in departure.

However, perhaps it is the ubiquitous and marked 'attraction to difference' that constitutes the most definitive aspect of existential migration and its distinction from conventional settled forms of life. In *Strangers to Ourselves*, Julia Kristeva offers a poetic text on foreignness, alternating between philosophy, cultural criticism, and depth analysis, by proclaiming 'the foreigner lives within us: he is the hidden face of our identity…'[76]. Yet the one who actually chooses to leave, according to Kristeva, is 'poorly loved', is 'inaccessible', a stranger to his mother, riveted to a certain and inaccessible elsewhere, he is indifferent to any pleas to stay and must seek an invisible 'beyond'. This foreigner has a perspective that makes everything, including himself, relative and indifferent, while the 'settled' are rutted in unacknowledged sediment, mediocre by comparison. In leaving home, the migrant transmutes discomfort into resistance. I will present a few instances where Kristeva's evocation touches the experiences of existential migration.

According to Kristeva, the foreigner does not emphasize the origin as much as others do. He has fled the origin though it continues to fester, pain, and enrich. The origin continues to haunt but it is the *elsewhere* or the *'nowhere* versus the roots' where he has invested his hopes. The universal need to belong is partially transferred from the origin to the cosmopolitan, the past to the future. The foreigner

---

76. Kristeva, 1991:1

challenges the identity of the group and of himself, mixing 'humility with arrogance, suffering with domination, a feeling of having been wounded and being all-powerful'. Kristeva depicts Freud's conception of the uncanny as a 'foreignness' that 'creeps into the tranquillity of reason itself... Henceforth, we know that we are foreigners to ourselves...'[77]. This re-working of traditional psychoanalysis brings us much closer to an existential dimension in which the uncanny or unheimlich is a part of our existence rather than a sign of repression or pathology.

Kristeva comes to the conclusion that 'To worry or to smile, such is the choice when we are assailed by the strange; our decision depends on how familiar we are with our own ghosts'. She also points out that it is surprising that foreigners are not explicitly mentioned in descriptions of the uncanny or unheimlich. She considers it quite plausible that xenophobia includes some attempt to negate the unheimlich. The foreigner reminds us of what we reject as strange within ourselves. In this formulation rejection of the foreigner (or presumably the outcast at home) can be thought of as the struggle to remain at home within ourselves by rejecting our own unfathomability. The uncanny strangeness of the foreigner comprises what in fact is the same between us; we are both foreign, to self and other – foreignness is the bedrock of the world, in which there is a momentary recognition that none of us belong. If the foreign is the basis of our commonality as well as the difference that distances us from each other, then we have discerned two definitions of 'foreign' – the existential in which the foreign is our founding commonality, and the neurotic, in which the foreign is created externally in the act of rejecting the mystery within one's own 'self'. This suggests a darker motivation within the home environment's designation of specific members as 'different' (foreign): Do these individuals, many of the participants in this research, surreptitiously threaten an unheimlich intrusion into established homiress? One can only speculate about this, but it suggests that existential migration offers

---

77. Kristeva, 1991: 170

a comment upon the particular environment that the migrant issued from as much as a description of the one who leaves (or was ejected).

Kristeva's account, beautiful and pessimistic, certainly describes some aspects of the experience of existential migration, yet leaves out others. She is an antidote to the unbalanced depiction of voluntary migration as all rosy postmodern potential, supplanting this scene with one of opaque hopelessness. She seems oblivious to the more positive and optimistic aspects of being a foreigner. However, her analysis does offer the following points to ponder:

1. Existential migrants display a drive towards future potential and a required escape from present captivity, both 'freedom-to' and 'freedom-from'.
2. The stranger is fascinated by an 'invisible beyond' (reminiscent of Heidegger), riveted by our hidden identity in the unheimlich. The primordial question of why some individuals have their attention diverted from the hearth is haunting and remains unanswered.
3. Kristeva's account implicates the homeworld as instrumental in the migrant's departure, they expel the migrant, they push out threatened contamination in a refusal to recognize the unheimlich and foreign within each person and in the midst of 'home'.
4. There have emerged two definitions of 'foreign' in parallel with the two-fold definitions of home, homelessness, and belonging. 'Foreign' can refer to an underlying existential commonality within each person as well as the manifestation of apparent 'difference'.

11.1 PRACTICAL IMPLICATIONS

Looking back, it appears that some people have always been in a process of existential migration, desperate to leave but patiently acquiring skills and adequate self-confidence to cope in unfamiliar settings. Many people left home in incrementally larger migrations, with a felt direction though often no clear goal. The process of 'existential migration' can pose as more superficial economic migration, concealing its deeper dimensions. Some participants valued their ability to adapt to foreign cultures while also recognizing that this malleability threatened their own sense of self. Participants often report comparing themselves to peers and family who stayed behind. Such comparison elicits complex feelings of superiority and envy. As participants age, some begin to desire the positive attributes of a settled life while also seeking to maintain their mobility and personal sensitivities. Many people end up feeling in a limbo state where no place will ever feel like home again and perhaps it is possible to accept this predicament as a way of life.

Numerous research studies have now been completed on the adjustment difficulties inherent in cross-cultural corporate relocations, concluding that a quarter of business managers undergo an unexpected *personal disturbance of some sort*. These individuals did not, for the most part, leave in order to develop nascent potentialities of being or to explore assumptive aspects of existence. However, these relocations are unsettling enough that a number of expatriate managers return to their home country prematurely and many leave their employment after returning from abroad. One study concludes that assigning expatriate managers to a superficially similar culture can cause even more disturbance than sending them to a very different culture[78]. These dynamics were eloquently explored in the participant stories, Sarah's among others. She proposed that in a very different culture the awareness of dissimilarity is in the forefront whereas if the culture at least superficially seems very similar, then dissonances are more difficult to notice or understand. Subsequently they get in deeper and play with one's identity. She also articulated the double-edged skill of adaptation and the inherent potential for fragmentation in a self that previously may have appeared whole. These issues demonstrate the potential for experiencing the unheimlich, finding the foreignness within, as indicated in the previous chapter. Such findings undermine any assumption that one can automatically remain *personally* unaffected

---

78   Selmer and Shiu, 1999

by international resettlement.

When it comes to returning home, contrary to expatriates' expectations, the return 'home' can be as challenging as another migration to a foreign country. Though this 'foreign' country is deeply familiar as well as unexpectedly strange. When studying the experience of return, researchers don't take account of the potential existential restlessness that may develop for the repatriate who has experienced foreignness. Though these authors contemplate the impact of superficial changes in behaviour and comportment from living abroad, they do not consider that these behavioural changes might express a far more fundamental shift in one's self and one's assumptions about the solidity of life. Having an opportunity to explore the deeper existential aspects of experiences abroad might actually result in increased self-understanding for these returnees. At least that was the effect for many of the participants who found the research interview transformative.

Some research suggests that individuals who are most successful at adjusting to a new culture are often much less successful at readjusting back to the original culture. It may be that 'adjustment' requires a person who is 'open' to alterity and ambiguity, and seeks stimulation, which is an apt though partial description of many of the participants.

The same person may re-adjust poorly upon returning home since the new ideas conflict with tradition. The returnee finds no internationally minded people, discovers that old friends are bored upon hearing accounts of the sojourn, and experiences no stimulation in the country which is already so well known. This relation between adaptation to the new and nonadaptation to the old is undoubtedly related to individual differences in *tolerant personality traits*. '*Tolerant people*' can benefit from both the old and the new and do not necessarily experience debilitating feelings of impotence upon returning to their home culture[79].

---

79. Brislin 1981:122, *italics added*

Unfortunately this term 'tolerant person' reduces the complexity of processes of identity, belonging, home, foreignness, and the unheimlich, to a hypothetical psychological *trait* called 'tolerance'. Remember Heidegger's accusation that we have forgotten '...the *proper* plight of dwelling as *the* plight...'? It strikes me as idyllic to suggest that there are 'tolerant people' who can even tolerate a lack of tolerance upon their return home. Are there, in reality, set *traits* enabling persons to adapt equally to the foreign and the traditionally familiar? The concept of existential migration, as presented, prioritizes person-world interactions over this idea of self-contained subjects with fixed psychic traits unaffected by diverse situations. Below is a brief exploration of what may constitute differences between the process conceptualization of existential migration and the trait-and-stage depiction evident in most acculturation research.

11.1.1 Stage Theories or Process?

The vast majority of research studies on acculturation and psychological difficulties in foreign adaptation remain couched within notions of generalized stage theories. The concept of 'culture shock' underscores most stage-based hypotheses and presumes that coping with difference causes a seismic fracture in identity, subverting it with self-doubt and insecurity, both of which are seen as problems to be solved. The transition of adapting across cultures has been hypothesized as fitting a W-curve: initial culture shock, adaptation, and then re-entry shock, characterized by negative experiences including pronounced stress, sleep deprivation, and confusion[80]. Not surprisingly, 're-entry shock' has also been characterized as having stages, including denial regarding the difficulty of reintegration, disillusionment, renewed commitment to realistic goals, self-confidence and resourcefulness, and the trimming of foreign-acquired behaviours and traits[81].

---

80. Brislin, 1981
81. Page, 1990

Peter Read, introduced earlier in the discussions of home, recounts that groups of immigrants arriving in Australia attracted the attention of 'an army of sociologists' who developed various theoretical models for how immigrants 'assimilate'.

> Such mechanistic models, which detected stages like 'naturalization', 'absorption', 'assimilation', and 'acculturation' were replaced by more sophisticated theories which allowed for individual difference, changing attitudes throughout the whole of life ... Immigration theorists now allow that the process of belonging in a new land is much more complex than previously imagined[82].

Despite Read's assurance, review of the literature reveals the continued preponderance of stage theories claiming that their findings are valid for everyone. The felt and evocative first-person narratives of migration are almost entirely absent, objectifying 'migrants' into a foreign species – suddenly it's about *them*, not *us*. The emphasis and method of my analysis stresses lived experience not theory. First of all, my 'process' emphasis avoids the prescriptive implications of stage theories, that there are sequential steps that individuals are expected to follow. 'Process' acknowledges the lived intricacies and vast diversity of human interaction and therefore offers no general predictions (not-being-at-home can lapse into being-at-home and vice versa), while implying that experience is never fully encapsulated by any theories. 'Stages' and 'traits' are supposedly discrete and discernable *within* an individual subject, while 'process' points to implicit flux that is never comprehensively described, with an unpredictable directionality (not expected to smoothly follow a sequence). The disadvantages of stage theories is that they are imposed upon individual experience, resulting in simplistic 'diagnoses' and predictions of 'risk factors', 'pathology', and so on. I hope that my analysis in this book contributes something to resurrecting the actual person underneath these generalizations.

---

82. Read, 1996: 27-8

The concept of 'culture shock' is also complicated by the numerous accounts of participants for whom difference and the unfamiliar is not shocking but stimulating and actively desired; the 'culturally shocking' is welcome. This is not to deny any manifestations of person-place dissonance, but for participants these are as likely to be experienced in the 'home' environment as in the foreign – why are there no studies of 'culture shock' in the home? A 'process' perspective does not presuppose which place is 'home' and which place is 'shocking'. There is no pre-set chronology, nothing on which to base judgements such as 'healthy' or 'pathological', except as experientially self-ascribed by the individual. Of course a migrant can say of him or her self, 'I feel good' or 'this feels uncomfortable to me'. Any individual may be in an interaction they would label as 'feeling at home' for years, before possibly returning to the homelessness and paradox of existential migration.

Though I'm indicating a distinction between existential migration and other modes of migration, it strikes me as possible that corporate relocations and the movement of refugees and exiled populations, though not instigated as existential journeys, could perhaps on some occasions *induce* individual processes of existential migration. Potentially any of us could succumb to, or embark upon, a *process* of existential migration, through choice, duress, and perhaps accidentally through career advancement in a foreign posting. In the most abstract, *a process of existential migration occurs when the interaction between person and place allows it, invites it, or demands it.* Even when 'demanded' or 'forced' as in exile, such a process can presumably be resisted by retreat into hominess and idealization of the lost place (or also perhaps into various 'problems in living' such as addictions and mental health issues).

11.1.2 Intercultural Training

Expatriate management assignments fail about fifty percent of the time. This has generated intercultural competency training focused on managers pre-departure, and includes raising cultural awareness, exposing trainees to assumptions of cross-cultural transitional 'stages', teaching trainees to understand how cultural differences influence our behaviour and offering briefings on the customs of specific countries prior to relocation. However, current practice in cross-cultural research and intercultural training is not sensitive enough to reveal the impact of *individual values* upon relocation 'success' because these values are usually implicit and easily obscured, requiring phenomenological unpacking through respectful dialogue. Pre-departure courses should incorporate self-reflective 'empathy training' rather than only the more knowledge-based deliveries, to facilitate favourable social contact with *individuals* in the new place and thus enhance adaptation. The field of intercultural training could be enhanced by an exploration of candidates' deeper orientations to living, their attitudes to belonging, independence, difference and similarity, and the meaningfulness of home, similar to the research described in this book. For example, training at present seems to be focused on lowering anxiety rather than exploring it, on making 'successful' adaptations rather than exploring life assumptions and one's reasons for leaving and whether, after exploring the possible ramifications, relocation really is the best option for each person. As a guess, I would speculate that 'existential migrants', with their developed adaptation capabilities and affinities for difference, might be well suited for international assignments, though the compatibility of such careers with values of freedom, independence, and self-actualization, might be more problematic in some cases.

CHAPTER 12
LEAVING AND INDIVIDUAL PSYCHOLOGY

Early family and peer relationships are frequently implicated in decisions to leave home or in the timing of the migration, however it is clear that reasons given for leaving are not necessarily causes of leaving. Individuals who acknowledge that early parental relationships had an impact on their leaving frequently cautioned that their feelings about home and travel cannot be reduced to only these dynamics. Difficult family circumstances seem to coalesce around pre-existing sensitivities in those who left, differentiating them from siblings who stayed. Relations with the original national culture and parental relations can become intermingled, so that an attitude of needing space from one is generalized to needing space from the other.

In order to label the motivations for migration, the psychoanalyst Michael Balint coined the term 'ocnophilic' for the tendency to hold onto what is certain and stable, and 'philobatic' to describe the tendency to seek out new and exciting experiences, situations, and places. Ocnophiles are characterized by their attachment to people, places, and objects and find it difficult to live alone. In contrast, philobats avoid ties and tend to live independently. They seek pleasure in adventures, voyages, new emotions, and are able to leave people and places behind without pain or sorrow. This theory has led some psychoanalysts to infer that ocnophiles have a pronounced affinity to remain rooted in their origins, abandoning them with difficulty. Philobats, in contrast, exhibit a tendency to migrate in pursuit of 'undiscovered horizons and new experience'[83]. These ideas are still based upon the assumption that the individual ideal is to be firmly rooted in a secure place.

The very few discussions of voluntary migration in the psychoanalytic literature do not recognize the *agony of choice* inherent in leaving nor the anguish of feeling pressured to return *exactly because* it is possible. The return home can be an attempt to prove that everything is still there, so it can be quite disorienting to find many things greatly changed. This can arouse feelings of pain and jealousy, as we've previously discussed, and an (unheimlich) feeling of strangeness, 'as if he were seeing the world from the perspective of the dead'[84]. The return home does not necessarily terminate the exhausting process of migration. The reality is yet another experience of being a stranger,

> …he sees the changes in people, things, habits and styles, houses and streets, relationships and affections… Not even his language sounds the same. Colloquialisms have changed, along with the tacit understanding of words, meanings, shared images, and past references, winks of complicity among the initiated – all the sublanguages that make up a language[85].

In 'The Uncanny', written in 1919, Freud distinguishes a class of frightening event which leads back to what is deeply familiar; something disturbing is seen where it is least expected. Feeling at home is both familiar *and* secretive, as in drawing the curtains to keep something private from the view of the neighbours. This is reminiscent of the insular home that our participants found suffocating. Not feeling at-home (unheimlich) is an experience of the unfamiliar and foreign rather than the hearth, with the implication of something

---

83. This discussion is from *Migration and Exile*, by Grinberg and Grinberg, 1989:21
84. Grinberg and Grinberg, 1989:183
85. Ibid: 186-7

secretive being revealed, opening the curtains. The uncanny thereby seems in fact to be a mix of the strange and the secret familiar in a process of revelation – the strange in the familiar or familiar in the strange. There are examples of this from the participant descriptions; uncomfortable experiences of *mis*appropriating a culture as similar to ones own only to find it is deeply but subtly unfamiliar, or accounts of returning home to find it changed, both signify an uncomfortable mélange of unexpected and familiar, stranger in a familiar land and local in a strange land.

Freud lists only a few specific situations that turn what is frightening into what is uncanny, and in Freud's description, returning home after some time in a foreign land or the anxiety of not feeling at home in the world, are peculiarly not amongst his examples. For Freud, anxiety signifies the presence of something repressed in the psyche, whereas for Heidegger anxiety is an existential given, a fact of the world. What makes the uncanny special cannot be a return of the repressed if what distinguishes it is *consciously felt*; though it is not clear, if it is felt, it is not unconscious. In light of the phenomenon of existential migration, it makes more obvious sense to explore an understanding of the unheimlich that is deeply *of* the world, not a product of unconscious pressure. In psychoanalysis, the uncanny loses its world significance and its universally shared potential. It is referred to as a 'state of disorganization', a kind of 'paralysis', leaving the person vulnerable to dissociation. It becomes a walled-off subjective disturbance and in this form, not related to the phenomenon of existential migration. Additionally, acculturation studies suggest that virtually anyone seems capable of commencing an experience of what I call existential migration, at least in the form of the unsettling reaction to international relocation. If, even in adulthood, anyone has the potential to experience the unheimlich dimension of migration, then it is in the order of an existential possibility rather than a developmental *disorder*.

12.1 PRELIMINARY THERAPEUTIC CONSIDERATIONS

Therapy with migrants has been focused primarily upon refugee populations, with the assumption that involuntary migrants are seen as more at-risk 'psychologically' than voluntary migrants. In these studies the refugee's lack of choice compared to the immigrant is a definitive component of their distress. If we are to challenge the bias towards settlement, we could say that it is the refugee's reluctance to loosen his or her grip, to let go into movement and the adventure of migration, that makes their displacement so disturbing.

A psychologist working with refugees, Renos Papadopoulos (mentioned previously), points out the curious situation in the psychotherapeutic literature that refugees, ostensibly people who have forcibly lost their homes, are primarily associated with issues of trauma rather than issues of home. He is the first to ask, 'If the main problem with refugees is their [forced] loss of home, why do they need psychotherapy?'[86]. In response, he posits that there are many forms of homecoming and perhaps therapy could be one of them.

One group of researchers have even argued that therapists in refugee transit camps must themselves have some idea of the 'psychological journey' involved in leaving home in order to react in a more than superficial way[87]. Presumably, openness to one's own issues of 'home' and personal reactions to homelessness is a crucial aspect of an empathetic response to refugees. Increased therapeutic sensitivity to the profundity of themes of home, loss of home, and homelessness, would certainly be a welcomed outcome of this book on existential migration. Given the characteristic sensitivities of existential migrants, it might seem reasonable to assume that a form of therapy offering a democratic and mutual dialogue incorporating exploratory space and freedom to construct one's own understandings instead of

---

86. Papadopoulos, 2002:3
87. Chan and Loveridge, 1987

imposing conventional theory might be appealing for this population. A practice I have called 'home-world dialogue', based upon an existential approach to therapy, is one attempt to offer this space.

Crucial features of existential migration are consistent with existential approaches to therapy[88], for example an emphasis on embodied experience of the world rather than theories of the unconscious or logical analysis of thoughts, a view of the self as process rather than fixed traits, a stance that doesn't diagnose or pathologize, and an emphasis on the implicit depth of the dilemmas of life with a tendency to value the mysterious, spiritual, 'unspeakable known' dimensions of existence. 'Home-world dialogues' may offer an invitation not only to those who have relocated internationally, but also to anyone interested in contemplating these aspects of life. Constructing therapeutic narratives around 'home' may assist work with refugees, migrant workers, international students, and individuals embarking upon intercultural relocations or recently returned from abroad, not to mention the promise of enhancing empathy in therapists working with such clients. The ambiguous identity of the 'homecomrade' suggests new thinking regarding the practice of 'cultural matching' in therapy, where therapists are often referred to clients based upon obvious cultural and ethnic similarities. At least in the case of individuals exhibiting aspects of existential migration, it seems plausible that these obvious bases for 'matching' may be counter-productive and that individual sensitivities such as those described by the participants might form a more appropriate basis for pairing these clients with empathetic therapists. The kind of therapist-client 'matching' I'm suggesting here might be considered a re-enactment of the person-environment matching that constitutes the experience of home, so that the therapeutic relationship offers an interaction in which, even momentarily, the *authentic* experience of home in the unheimlich may become manifest, for both participants.

---

88. For a comparison and summary, see Mick Cooper's *Existential Therapies*, 2003

CHAPTER 13
EXISTENTIAL MIGRATION AND AUTOBIOGRAPHIES OF EXILE

The interview excerpts reported in the first part of this book may constitute the first recorded biographies describing existential migrations. However, it is not uncommon for migrants to exhibit an aesthetic dimension, for example the migratory 'view from afar' which characterizes a whole genre of modern literature. The writer Andre Aciman edited a collection of writers' personal experiences of migration, but in his text an account of 'existential migration' is conspicuous by its absence. The closest we get is to cut and paste bits from accounts of the exile, the expatriate, and the émigré, in order to approximate the story of an existential migrant. For example Aciman makes a distinction between 'uprooted' and 'unrooted' pointing to those without roots, as distinct from those whose roots have been ripped up and left dangling. Those without roots, the 'permanent transients' resemble the experience of an existential migrant. But it is not accurate to say that the participants (and myself) have *no* roots – if that were true presumably we could settle anywhere and nowhere and we may not even comprehend the issue of 'home' at all. But as Renata described, one wants roots of some kind. One begins to sink them in a new place where the ground is inevitably stony, maybe we can grow around the stones or maybe the earth is impenetrable. Part of the stoniness surely is the fact that the new ground is not the familiar ground of home. We had *something* there, perhaps only shallow ambivalent roots but at least something specific making that ground forever unique.

Aciman suggests that 'When exiles [forced or voluntary] see one place they're also seeing – or looking for – another behind it. Everything bears two faces, everything is shifty because everything is mobile…'[89]. He describes how the exile examines each alien land to assess whether it could become his, or hers, and that this process never terminates, but continues even after a 'good enough' place is found. Aciman reveals that in his case, he experiences a strong desire for *everything* to remain the same, stressing that this is '… typical of people who have lost everything, including their roots or their inability to grow new ones…'[90] Yet from the interviews we read two simultaneous impulses, the desire for the 'homeland' to remain unchanged, even if one could never envisage living there again, and the personal *attraction* to dynamic diversity, continual foreignness. It seems that existential migration often includes this dynamic of being attracted to exploration, 'perpetual transition' in Aciman's words, while maintaining contact, though at some distance, with the homeworld. In certain manifestations, existential migration may be conceived fancifully as a mode of *failed time travel*. It is inseparably future-oriented while sometimes past-obsessed, and often cyclical, continually circling while arriving nowhere. Aciman's account also discerns '*root envy*' in exilic and existential migration; the envy of another's solidity in the world as amply suggested in the research interviews. Such envy arises from a distance but on closer inspection its flip side arises: to witness the daily routines required to tend those roots often triggers the repulsion for settled life.

The writer Eva Hoffman was a Polish teenager who was brought to Canada by her family. She does not exemplify voluntary migration

---

89. Aciman, 1999: 13
90. Ibid:21

but she does hauntingly describe relevant aspects of migration that contrast with, and sometimes compliments, the existential migrant. Her autobiography, *Lost in Translation. A Life in a New Language* is a beautiful homage to the particulars of love, hate, and disorientation entailed in an un-chosen leave-taking and grudging adaptation. Hoffman makes an evocative appeal to the universality of these experiences,

> We feel ejected from our first homes and landscapes, from childhood, from our first family romance, from our authentic self. We feel there is an ideal sense of belonging, of community, of attunement with others and at-homeness with ourselves, that keeps eluding us ... On one level, exile is a universal experience[91].

Hoffman lists the significant positive effects of exile, including 'a certain fertile detachment' giving one creative new ways of seeing, a confrontation with aspects of life that otherwise would remain obscure, an opportunity to explore 'fundamental problems' from another vantage point.

> Exile places one at an oblique angle to one's new world and makes every emigrant, willy-nilly, into an anthropologist and relativist; for to have a deep experience of two cultures is to know that no culture is absolute – it is to discover that even the most interstitial and seemingly natural aspects of our identities and social reality are constructed rather than given and that they could be arranged, shaped, articulated in quite another way[92].

However, Hoffman is concerned about the inversion of values occurring in our postmodern world, where everything is relative and displacement celebrated. She is not convinced that 'uncertainty, displacement, fragmented identity' can be transmuted into victories. She believes this positioning, 'underestimates the sheer human cost of actual exile as well as some of its psychic implications...' In other words, something is lost in our loss of 'loss'. If this postmodern future is actualized, how would we even express those aspects of our human

---

91. Hoffman, 1989:40
92. Ibid:51

condition that we can currently refer to as existential issues of home; the unheimlich, quest for identity, the call to actualize our potential, our need for some kind of belonging…

> Real dislocation, the loss of all familiar external and internal parameters, is not glamorous, and it is not cool. It is a matter not of wilful psychic positioning but of an upheaval in the deep material of the self[93].

In this emerging world, change will come as surely to those who stay put in their sameness as to those who are mobilized by the requirements of a globalized world economy. We've already witnessed extreme nationalist reactions to these trends, perhaps partly due to the intrusion of Otherness into 'home conceived of mostly as a conservative site of enclosure and closure, of narrow-mindedness, patriarchal attitudes, and dissemination of nationalism'[94]. This *excessive* at-homeness, over-determined by the need for security in an increasingly groundless existence, is a stagnant pool cut off from the ebb and flow of the world. Hoffman expresses her experience of loss by quoting the following poem, 'A Room and a Half', by Brodsky[95]:

> For a while he is absorbed with new vistas,
> absorbed with building his own nest,
> with manufacturing his own reality. Then
> one day, when the new reality is mastered,
> when his own terms are implemented,
> he suddenly learns that his old nest is gone,
> that those who gave him life are dead. On
> that day he feels like an effect suddenly
> without a cause… What he can't blame on
> nature is the discovery that his achievement,
> the reality of his own manufacture, is less
> valid than the reality of his abandoned nest.
> *That if there ever was any-thing real in his
> life, it was precisely that nest, oppressive and
> suffocating, from which he so badly wanted
> to flee.* He knows how willful, how intended

---

93. Hoffman, 1999:50
94. Ibid:58
95. Brodsky, 1986: Section 18, *italics added*

and premeditated everything that he has manufactured is. How, in the end, all of it is provisional.

In her experience of being brought to a foreign land as part of a family migration Hoffman seems *pushed* into a process of existential migration that would not have been her wont had she been left to live her adolescent years into adulthood in her native Poland. She expresses her need to lessen her alienation and to belong, to 'bend toward another culture without falling over', to settle in order to achieve the precondition for 'gravity' that she as an individual requires. Unlike our participants, she left her home 'regretfully' and brokenhearted yet she is able to appreciate some ecstatic and creative moments that this process offers her,

> But as the plane lifts above the cloud line, there is the heady pleasure that repeats itself every time I travel. The whole world lies below me, waiting for articles to be written about it. There is the great ocean below, and the great sky above, and nothing between me and pure possibility[96].

There are only hints in Hoffman's autobiographies of the unnoticed migrants who pass through ports and arrival lounges alone, who chose to leave in order to express or to address something about life itself, the young gay man or lesbian, the first-born, the youngest or only child who never quite fit in, the child smothered by expectation, the gifted and the oddballs, the sister intent on impressive success, the outsiders who usually arrive one by one and have no one to meet them on their arrival. I suspect that such 'undocumented' migrations in fact constitute a small but continuous current in an alternative human history. A history that would tell a very different story of humanity.

The influential cultural studies theorist Edward Said, in contrast to Hoffman, presents feelings and experiences more representative of many of the participants. He was an exile, an expatriate, and an

---

96. Hoffman, 1999: 253

immigrant. He recounts his leaving in his memoir *Out of Place* and a few personal essays, for example 'No Reconciliation Allowed',

> For as long as I can remember, I had allowed myself to stand outside the umbrella that shielded or accommodated my contemporaries. Whether this was because I was genuinely different, objectively an outsider, or because I was temperamentally a loner I cannot say, but the fact is that although I went along with all sorts of institutional routines because I felt I had to, something private in me resisted them. I don't know what it was that caused me to hold back, but even when I was most miserably solitary or out of synch with everyone else, I held onto this private aloofness very fiercely. I have envied many friends... who had lived in the same place all their lives, or who had done well in accepted ways, or who truly belonged, but I do not recall ever thinking that any of that was possible for me. It wasn't that I considered myself special, but rather that I didn't fit the situations I found myself in and wasn't too displeased to accept this state of affairs[97].

Said echoes many of the interviews by emphasizing that 'always' there was something different about him. In response he tried to clothe himself in the expectations of his family and culture. Unlike Hoffman, Said stands in favour of the postmodern values of 'contingency'. Speaking simply from his own life experience, he accepts the 'provisional satisfaction which is quickly ambushed by doubt' as *personally* preferable to the 'sleep of self-satisfaction' he perceives in settlement. It may be significant that Said's journey occurs at an age where he was old enough to 'choose' his imposed departure. Being sent to school in America began a long period of loneliness and unhappiness but it also initiated the arc of his life by liberating him from an oppressive homeworld. He, like the participants in this study, feels the 'anxious moodiness of travel' as well as a form of envy for those who remain settled and unscathed by dislocation. Said never really 'settled', even after nearly forty years of living in New York he described his tenure there as provisional. He preferred motion and being slightly 'out of place' to the self with gravity, with a firmly rooted centralized life theme. In *Reflections on Exile and other Literary and Cultural Essays*, Said presents the darker side of his experience,

---

97. Said, 1999b:102-3

> Exile is strangely compelling to think about but terrible to experience. It is the unhealable rift forced between a human being and a native place, between the self and its true home: its essential sadness can never be surmounted. And while it is true that literature and history contain heroic, romantic, glorious, even triumphant episodes in an exile's life, these are no more than efforts meant to overcome the crippling sorrow of estrangement. The achievements of exile are permanently undermined by the loss of something left behind forever[98].

Said points out that much of contemporary western culture includes migrations that are easier to document and thus easier to credit than the solitary migrations whose less tangible motivations dissipate when compared to newsworthy international turmoil. What is the contribution to society of those of us who have always been on the edge of belonging? Can this way of being, these 'existential sensitivities', offer anything to academia, the intelligentsia, aesthetics, spirituality, business, or politics? If, as many commentators have concluded, this is the 'age of the dispossessed', are those of us who embody *dispossession* better positioned to describe this process and to conceptualize the consequences? The tables are turning and one question is whether 'existential migrants' are able to chronicle this new inversion for the many who are unwittingly about to embark upon it.

Charles Simic, cast out of Belgrade as a child, recounts the 'treacheries and horrors' that eventually resulted in his family landing on the shores of eastern America. His story is one of total disenfranchisement, brutal bureaucrats, and dehumanizing border crossings. This phase of the refugee's flight is the antithesis of the concept of existential migration; no ability to pursue one's own individual potential, no opportunity to exercise the sometimes painful but precious need for independence, or freedom or choice. 'Immigration, exile, being uprooted and made a pariah may be the most effective way yet devised to impress on an individual the arbitrary nature of his or her own existence'[99]. However, as a young sixteen-year-old boy newly settled in New York

---

98. Said, 2000:173
99. Simic,1999:123-4

with his family, Simic's experience suggests that individual migration may supersede the fixed 'categories' (refugee, exile, migrant worker, émigré, existential migrant) and that these categories should perhaps be held lightly, taken less substantively. Simic's response to his refugee status was the converse of Hoffman's experience (she also relocated as a teenager) and was nothing short of enthusiastic,

> It sounds nice intellectually to claim that an expatriate can never feel at home anywhere again. It's definitely not true of a sixteen year old. I was more adaptable than a cat or a goldfish would have been. I was eager to see and taste everything[100].

Simic's fellow 'homecomrades' spent their time soaked in nostalgia, imaging their triumphant return home when the grafted Communist regime would inevitably topple. But, interestingly, Simic's response to this new world was not a longing for the old, but rather a kind of individual re-evaluation similar to the narratives of our participants,

> It's terrible when collective sentiments one is born with begin to seem artificial, when one starts to suspect that one's exile is a great misfortune but also a terrific opportunity to get away from everything one has always secretly disliked about the people one grew up with.[101]

America gave Simic an opportunity to free himself from socially assigned roles that would have quickly descended upon him in his home country. New York gave him a welcome exposure to many other cultures and ways of life. His openness to this diversity produced in him the sense of being a 'free individual', with a clearer idea of the workings of the world and of his own preferences; 'I prefer that solitary knowledge to the jubilation of the masses in Red Square or at some Nuremberg rally'. Of course these are extremes few would readily associate with, but Simic's way of being independent was not a superficial response to the excesses of right or left. He developed into an acclaimed American lyric poet, describing this form of verse as,

---

100. Ibid: 127
101. Simic, 1999:129

> ... the voice of a single human being taking stock of his or her own existence... The poem is both a part of history and outside its domain. That is its beauty and its hope. A poet is a member of that minority that refuses to be part of any official minority...[102].

Reading these words it is tempting to speculate regarding Simic's pre-existing proclivities before being displaced as a refugee. His sentiments certainly converge with the felt experience of many of the participants. He reminds us that even amongst refugee populations, there may be a few individuals who secretly taste freedom rather than loss in their forced evacuation from home.

These evocative autobiographies by literary figures and their reflections on home and migration echo many of the themes and concepts elaborated in this book. Perhaps future volumes of exilic and migratory literature might include an account of 'existential migration' with its discernable motivations for leaving home and its recognizable sensitivities toward being.

---

102. Ibid: 135

CHAPTER 14
FINAL CAUTIONARY THOUGHTS

This book is based upon the stories that people tell about their own motivations for leaving home and the experiences that ensue. It is a first attempt to present the unacknowledged importance of existential motives in migration as they were discovered through these stories. Existential migration emphasizes psychological, philosophical and spiritual motivations for the journey that originates from 'home' in the traditional sense in search of 'authentic home' in the existential sense. The traditional home is characterized by its coziness, rooted in place, while the authentic home nurtures an experience of dwelling where we belong without exiling the deeply human sense of not-being-at-home in the world.

Existential migration offers; an ethical sensitivity to difference, a future-orientation that includes melancholia, and a pronounced individualism. It reveals definitions of home, homelessness, belonging, and foreignness, which are the binary opposites of our usual understandings of these terms. One potent example of this is that 'home' in its conventional sense may in fact constitute 'true exile' from the mystery of existence. These new definitions illustrate the deeper universal significance that may rest at the heart of individual experiences of relocation. I propose that existential migrants comprise a permeable *alternative human history*, unrecorded and unacknowledged until now. And even now, by its nature, this 'history' remains translucent and furtive.

My hope is that this book might also constitute an introduction to the intense dilemmas and emotional potency of *voluntary* migration in general – that choosing to leave does not eradicate the sense of loss and distress so readily acknowledged in other forms of cross-cultural relocation. Although existential migration has diverse origins and trajectories, the participants in this study describe a number of remarkably consistent themes and specific sensitivities. Despite such consistency, this form of migration has not been visible enough to be previously recognized. So it remains possible that existential migration is an unacknowledged strain within many migrations that masquerade under more commonly ascribed motivations.

Existential migration can be expressed as an organizing *way of being* for some individuals, while for other people it may form a minor 'strand' within a way of being characterized by other main features. As alluded to previously, a process of existential migration may commence unbidden within experiences of forced exile or economic relocations; usurping the original motivations with an unexpected revelation of deeply unsettling realities. To reiterate, this is a self-ascribed *process* not a diagnosis. And my intuition is that a number of individuals who have left their homelands to live as foreigners will, to varying degrees, recognize themselves in these pages, and feel affected by the stories and ideas described in this book. This is yet to be seen.

Other outstanding questions remain: what becomes of individuals who would subscribe to a process of existential migration but who cannot, due to commitments, or for economic or political reasons, leave home? And to what extent are the premises of this study also translatable to portions of the settled population? During my studies I have found that nearly everyone I've spoken to has a uniquely emotional response to questions about home, belonging, and difference, regardless of their position on the continuum of sedentary to transient. I have had conversations about the meaning of home with strangers on trains, with acquaintances at professional conferences, with students, friends, and colleagues. Whether the person has left home to become a foreigner, or not, each seems able to readily recount deeply felt constellations of home. Ask about 'home' and the likely response, I've found, is an emotional dip into personal biography. There appears to be *something* universal in narratives of home, and this book testifies to the fact that although choosing to leave home is a unique experience, it offers a comment on the significance of human dwelling generally, and as such potentially raises questions for any human being.

This research originated from contemplating my response to that early morning view over Calcutta. Since then this work has itself been a fascinating personal journey. As I edit these final lines I am again sitting in the departure lounge at Kathmandu airport, seven years after that first journey. During this time not only did I learn intimate details about others' lives, but I also learned a great deal about my own struggles to belong some where or some way. The hiatus in Budapest remains a potent memory of dislocation and self-reflection, due in part to the intensity of analyzing and living the same process simultaneously. To this day I have yet to return to that city – I feel it will require courage to do that, to acknowledge that I actually lived there. I now realize how difficult it is for me to return to places I've lived, at least until a certain period of time has passed and the emotional resonances have begun to fade. Returning to these 'foster' homes, and there have been a few for me and perhaps for you, initiates feelings of loss that can be almost unbearable – it's like witnessing a death I've never had permission to grieve, like finding an unburied corpse that points an accusing finger directly at me. As a result of the changes in me during the process of researching this topic, I decided to return to my origin in Canada, in fact to teach at the university where I was an undergraduate twenty years before. I lasted eighteen months. I have no doubt that I needed to return but it did not take long for me to realize that I did not need to stay. In retrospect I think I needed to bury the dead, so-to-speak. Or to try to sew together two discontinuous lives in order to feel that they were in fact lived by the same person, and took place during the same epoch, on the same planet. I've been back in London for nearly two years now and for the first time in my life there is a new feeling of peace, of *settling* in some subtle but significant way. Probably not in the way that my neighbours feel settled and certainly not the way my parents have always been settled, deeply rooted and interwoven into the web of lives around them. My 'settled' has come about largely through a gradual acceptance of my homelessness. I have freed myself from the assumption that I must be place-specific in my attachment to this earth. This acceptance is not without loss, longing, and envy. I have given up on a type of belonging that is not mine to have and thereby paradoxically achieved at least some form of belonging.

I wonder about the countless young professionals who are expected to take advantage of this new borderless world by furthering their careers with a stint abroad. What is the impact of this international mobility on them? Having seen a number of these corporate globalizers during the course of my work as a psychologist in London, I am convinced that this relocation is usually not without personal impact. There is much more involved than simply swapping one country and one city for another, simply changing the familiar brands of milk and cereal for new ones with different labels. For some of these young professionals their unsettledness presumably subsides eventually when they return home. For others, who knows?

Along with expectations of mobility, globalization also demands rapid homogenization. Will increasing familiarity mean that we will all come to be at home everywhere, surrounded by the same reassuring customs and commodities no matter where we go? Will it mean no more moments of *relief* on Calcutta rooftops? Are we witnessing the eradication of global difference along with the awareness that this loss even matters? It may be quite appealing and comforting to *some* people to consider a planet where *other* people are bent towards their familiar world and their taken-for-granted everyday habits. So while a few economically powerful cultures spread their version of cozy familiarity all around the world, the implicit consequence is that others will experience 'culture shock' at home as internationalism replaces local values, customs, and commerce. I suspect we've only begun to see this process, and the backlash against it is already being played out around the globe as evident in our news headlines. Change is happening; either due to the expectation that one will live abroad for some of ones adult life or because of the rapid intrusion of internationalism into even the most homogenous provincial places.

Another aspect of this process is less visible but perhaps even more serious. When the dust settles perhaps it is not some incarnation of global hominess that will appear but rather the dawning realization that no one really belongs anywhere on earth anymore. That we have achieved a world where precious little *real* difference is left. In place of the alien we have only the superficially unfamiliar, few opportunities to be unsettled and inspired by confrontation with the strange or the unheimlich. Finding the question of 'how to dwell' will be a great challenge if people are no longer able to come 'home', or 'belong' except in the most tawdry sense of those words. Without the authentic call for 'homecoming' we will have achieved the end of belonging. No one will really belong anywhere anymore. 'Belonging', like the diagnosis of nostalgia and homesickness, will be consigned to the annals of human history, replaced by new diagnoses for the human condition.

If that is the psychological consequence of our current rush to globalization we will truly be lost. But in these concerns about what the future holds, the experiences of existential migrants may offer some hope. These stories serve as parables for the future and as such they offer a warning to us all. They awaken us to consideration of the deeper psychological impact of what is now presented as mere economic necessity. Through considering the experiences in Part One, we can begin to find ways of living with, rather then mindlessly attempting to eradicate, our unsettledness and our longing to find a way to dwell in this mysterious world. And still for some of us the ideal is not to be at home, but to be longing for home, forever on the way home. That feeling, that tragic sublime homelessness, is where we feel most alive, and where we most belong.

BIBLIOGRAPHY

Aciman, Andre (Ed.) (1999) *Letters of Transit. Reflections on Exile, Identity, Language, and Loss.* New York: The New York Press

Aronowitz, Michael (1984) The Social and Emotional Adjustment of Immigrant Children: A Review of the Literature. *International Migration Review*, 18 (2): 237-257

Baker, Khawla Abu (1999) Acculturation and Reacculturation Influence: Multilayer Contexts in Therapy. *Clinical Psychology Review.* 19 (8): 951-967

Baldursson, Stefan (2002) The Nature of At-Homeness. *Phenomenology Online.* Textorium Research Paper: 2-9, http://www.phenomenologyonline.com/articles/template.cfm?ID=264 (Accessed 8/09/03)

Balint, Michael (1959) *Thrills and Regressions.* New York: International U Press

Black, Richard (2002) Conceptions of 'home' and the political geography of refugee repatriation: between assumption and contested reality in Bosnia-Herzegovina. *Applied Geography*, 22: 123-38

Bowlby, J (1979) *The Making and Breaking of Affectional Bonds.* London: Tavistock

Brislin, Richard W (1981) *Cross-Cultural Encounters. Face-to-Face Interaction.* Needham Heights MA: Allyn and Bacon

Brislin, Richard W (1990) *Applied Cross-Cultural Psychology.* Cross-cultural Research and Methodology Series Vol. 14. Newbury Park CA: Sage Publications

Brodsky, Joseph (1986) *Less Than One: Selected Essays.* New York: Farrar, Straus and Giroux

Buber, Martin (1948) *The Way of Man.* London: Taylor and Francis

Campbell, Joseph (2004) *The Hero With a Thousand Faces.* New Jersey: Princeton University Press

Chan, Kwok B and Loveridge, David (1987) Refugees 'in transit': Vietnamese in a Refugee Camp in Hong Kong. *International Migration Review*, 21 (3): 745-759

Cooper, Mick (2003) *Existential Therapies*. London: Sage

Dallmayr, Fred (1993) *The Other Heidegger*. Ithaca NY: Cornell University Press

Fischer, Peter A; Martin, Reiner; & Straubhaar, Thomas (1997) Should I stay or should I go? In Hammar, Thomas; Brochmann, Grete; Tamas, Kristof; and Faist, Thomas (Eds.) (1997) *Immobility and Development*. Oxford UK: Berg: 49-90

Fjellestad, Danuta (1995) The insertion of the self into the space of borderless possibility: Eva Hoffman's exiled body... *Melus*, 20: 133- 151

Freud, Sigmund (1919) The Uncanny. Trans. James Strachey. In *The Standard Edition of the Complete Psychological Works of Sigmund Freud* (1955): 219-252. Vol. XVIII (1917-1919) An Infantile Neurosis and Other Works. London: Hogarth Press.

Gray, Glen J (1951) The idea of death in existentialism. *J of Philsophy*, 48 (5): 113-27

Graybeal, Jean (1990) *Language and the Feminine in Nietzsche and Heidegger*. Bloomington Ind: Indiana U Press

Grinberg, Leon and Grinberg, Rebeca (1989) *Migration and Exile*. London: Yale U Press.

Hammar, Thomas; Brochmann, Grete; Tamas, Kristof; and Faist, Thomas (Eds.) (1997) *Immobility and Development*. Oxford UK: Berg

Hammar, Thomas & Tamas, Kristof (1997) Why do people go or stay? In Hammar, Thomas; Brochmann, Grete; Tamas, Kristof; and Faist, Thomas (Eds.) (1997a) *Immobility and Development*. Oxford UK: Berg Publ.

Heidegger, Martin (1961) *An Introduction to Metaphysics*. (Trans. Ralph Manheim). New York: Doubleday

Heidegger, Martin (1962) *Being and Time*. (trans. J. Macquarrie, and E. Robinson,) New York: Harper and Row

Heidegger, Martin (1964) *Basic Writings* (2nd Ed. Rev.) (Ed. David Farrell Krell). New York: Routledge

Heidegger, Martin (1968) *What is called thinking?* Fred D Wieck and J Glenn Gray (trans.) New York: Harper and Row

Heidegger, Martin (1969) *Identity and Difference*. tr. Joan Stambaugh. New York: Harper and Row Torchbooks.

Heidegger, Martin (1971) *On the Way to Language*. New York: Harper and Row

Heidegger, Martin (1971a) *Poetry, Language, and Thought*. New York: Harper

Heidegger, Martin (1975) *Early Greek Thinking. The Dawn of Western Philosophy*. (Trans. David Krell & Frank Capuzzi). San Francisco: Harper and Row

Heidegger, Martin (2001) *Zollikon Seminars. Protocols, Conversations, Letters* (Ed. Medard Boss, Trans. Franz Mayr and Richard Askay). Evanston Ill: Northwestern U Press

Heidegger, Martin (1996) *Being and Time. A Translation of Zein und Zeit*. (trans. Joan Stambaugh). Albany NY: SUNY Press

Hoffman, Eva (1989) *Lost in Translation: A Life in a New Language*. New York: EE Dutton

Hoffman, Eva (1998) *Lost in Translation. A Life in a New Language*. London: Vintage Books

Hoffman, Eva (1999) 'The New Nomads', in A. Aciman (ed) *Letters of Transit. Reflections on Exile, Identity, Language, and Loss*. New York: The New York Press: 37-63

Huntington, June (1981) Migration as a Part of Life Experience. Paper presented at the *NSW Institute of Psychiatry, Seminar in Cross-Cultural Therapy*, October 22.

Iyer, Pico (2000) *The Global Soul. Jet-lag, shopping malls and the search for home*. London: Bloomsbury Publishing plc.

Kreisler, Henry (2000) Conversation with Eva Hoffman. *Conversations with History Series*. Institute of International Studies. U of C, Berkeley: http://globetrotter.berkeley.edu/people/Hoffman/hoffman-con3.html, (Accessed 21/03/05)

Kristeva, Julia (1986) A new type of intellectual: The dissident. *The Kristeva Reader*. Tori Moi (Ed.). London: Blackwell

Kristeva, Julia (1991) *Strangers to Ourselves*. New York: Cambridge University Press

Kruks, Sonia (1990) *Situation and Human Existence. Freedom, Subjectivity, and Society*. London: Unwin Hyman Ltd.

Lawrence, DH (1955) *Kangaroo*. London: Heineman

Leong, Chan-Hoong and Ward, Colleen (2000) Identity conflict in sojourners. *International Journal of Intercultural Relations*, 24: 763-776

Malkki, Liisa H (1995) Refugees and Exile: From "Refugee Studies" to the National Order of Things. *Annual Review of Anthropology*, 24: 495-523

Marcus, Clare Cooper (1995) *House as a Mirror of Self – Exploring the Deeper Meaning of Home*. Berkeley, CA: Conari Press

Marris, P (1974) *Loss and Change*. London: Routledge

Massey, Dorothy (1992) 'A Place Called Home'. *New Formations*, 17 (Summer): 3-15

O'Donohue, John (1998) *Eternal Echoes. Exploring our Hunger to Belong*. London: Bantam Books

Paasi, Anssi (1999) Boundaries as Social Processes: Territoriality in the World of Flows. *Geopolitics*, 3(1): 69-88.

Pain, Stephanie (2003) Dying to go home. *New Scientist*, July 19: 48-9

Papadopoulos, Renos K (ed.) (2002) *Therapeutic Care for Refugees. No Place Like Home*. The Tavistock Clinic Series. London: Karnac

Pattison, George (2000) *The Later Heidegger*. London: Routledge

Pictet, Dariane (2001) An inquiry into primordial thinking with Parmenides and Heidegger. *J of the Soc. of Exist. Anal.* 12.1: 33-47

Rapport, Nigel and Dawson, Andrew (1998) *Migrants of Identity. Perceptions of Home in a World of Movement*. Oxford: Berg Publ.

Rapport, Nigel (2003) *I Am Dynamite. An Alternative Anthropology of Power*. London: Routledge

Rea, Michael H (2000) A *furusato* away from home. *Annals of Tourism Research*. 27 (3): 638-660

Read, Peter (1996) *Returning to Nothing. The Meaning of Lost Places.* Cambridge: The Press Syndicate U of Cambridge

Ritivoi, Andreea Decui (2002) *Yesterday's Self. Nostalgia and the Immigrant Identity.* Oxford: Rowman and Littlefield

Rivett, Carole (date unknown) Returning to nothing; the meaning of lost places. *Bereavement Volunteer*, San Remo Community Health Centre, Victoria, Australia.

Said, Edward (1999a) *Out of Place*. London: Granta Books

Said, Edward (1999b) 'No Reconciliation Allowed', in A. Aciman (ed) *Letters of Transit. Reflections on Exile, Identity, Language, and Loss.* New York: The New York Press: (88-114)

Said, Edward (2000) *Reflections on Exile and other Literary and Cultural Essays.* London: Granta Books

Sato, Toru and McCann, Doug (1998) Individual Differences in Relatedness and Individuality: An exploration of two constructs. *Person. Individ. Diff.* 24 (6): 847-59

Schutz, A. (1964). The stranger: An essay in social psychology. *Collected papers II: Studies in social theory* (pp. 91-105). The Hague: Martinus Nijhoff.

Schutz, A. (1971) The Homecomer. *Collected Papers II.* The Hague: Martinus Nijhoff.

Selmer, Jan and Shiu, Lewis S.C. (1999) Coming Home? Adjustment of Hong Kong Chinese expatriate business managers assigned to the People's Republic of China. *Int. J. Intercultural Rel.*, 23 (3): 447-465

Shaw, Stephen (2002) Returning Home. *Phenomenology Online*. Textorium Research Paper: 1-10, http://www.phenomenologyonline.com/articles/shaw.html, (Accessed 11/09/03)

Shiraev, Eric and Levy, David (2001) *Introduction to Cross-cultural Psychology. Critical thinking and contemporary applications.* Boston: Allyn and Bacon

Simic, Charles (1999) 'Refugees', in A. Aciman (ed) *Letters of Transit. Reflections on Exile, Identity, Language, and Loss.* New York: The New York Press: (115-135)

Singh, Sagar (2002) Love, Anthroplogy, and Tourism. *Annals of Tourism Research*, 29 (1): 261-64

Steinbock, Anthony J (1995) *Home and Beyond. Generative Phenomenology after Husserl.* Evanston Ill: Northwestern University Press

Tolkien, JRR (1967) *The Return of the King. The Lord of the Rings Part III.* London: Harper Collins Publishers

van Manen, Max (1997) *Researching Lived Experience: Human Science for an Action Sensitive Pedagogy.* London, ON: The Althouse Press.

van Manen, Max Ed. (2002) *Writing in the Dark: Phenomenological Studies in Interpretive Inquiry.* London , ON: The Althouse Press. 1

Wang, Ning (1999) Rethinking authenticity in tourism experience. *Annals of Tourism Research*, 26(2): 349-70

Warminski, Andrzej (1990) Monstrous History: Heidegger Reading Holderlin. *Yale French Studies*, Volume 0, Issue 77: 193-209

Weber, Zita (2000) From assimilation to multiculturalism: Making sense of post-war migrants' experiences. *National Assoc. for Loss and Grief (VIC) Newsletter*, Winter Issue, June 2000: 7-11.

Winning, Anne (2002) Homesickness. Phenomenology Online. Textorium Research Paper: 1-11, http://www.phenomenologyonline.com/articles/winning.html, (Accessed 05/09/03)

INDEX

A

accents
  and sameness 53
acculturation 133
acculturation research 190
Aciman, Andre 199
adaptability 133
adaptation 193
  as skill and threat 188
adapting 117
addiction 177, 192
adolescence 24, 53, 63, 90
adopted 24
  country 46
adventure 165, 177
aesthetic 53, 199
afraid 36
age-appropriate 111
aging 95, 111
airports 10
alien 161, 164
alienated 50
alienation 164
  at home 53
alienworld 159, 161
alternative human history 7, 162, 203, 209
ambiguity 36
ambivalence 38
ambivalent
  about belonging at home 54
anaesthetized 25
analysis 27
  in Budapest 35
anchor 37
anonymity 77
anthropologist 16, 95, 165
anthropology 106
anxiety 23, 169, 193, 196

assimilate 55
assimilation 46, 133
assumptions 73
  about identity 47
asthma 59
attachment 148
attachments
  to place 145
authentic 159
authentic communication 143
authentic unheimlich 176
authorities 62
autobiographies 199, 203
autonomous 157
awareness 170

B

backlash 176
Balint, Michael 23, 194
being alone 58
Being and Time 24
being-at-home 93
being at home in oneself 96
belong 159
belonging 16, 42, 60, 131, 137, 178
  ambivalence of 47
  conditional 48
  through return 95
bereavement 20
biographical 77
birthplace 160
birthright
  to land 46
bodily comportment 160
bonds 154

border crossings 10
borderless world 211
boredom 165
boundaries 130
Bowlby 21
Brislin 190
Budapest 34
bullied 50
Bush, George 161
business managers 188

C

Calcutta 8
call 107
calling 68
call of conscience 171
Campbell, Joseph 180
Canadian
  as example of identity 43
capitalist 15
causal explanations 50, 82, 87
censor 55
censorship 75
challenge 77
childhood 83, 89, 144
  preparation to leave 106
childhood possessions 94
childhood residence 160
children 78, 116
choice 19, 61, 79, 158, 195
  importance of 65
choosing
  to exist 88
cities 94
claustrophobia 48
comfort zone 66
coming to be at home 175

commercial 176
communicate 79
community 7, 49, 50, 131, 147
compatriots 21
compliance 59
concrete
  thinking as 153
conflict 59
conform 45, 88
conformist 77
conservative 79
consumerism 164
consumerist 25
containment 21, 148
contemporary worldview 164
contradictions 115
conventional 10, 25, 68
  spiritual beliefs 69
Cooper, Mick 198
corporate relocations 188
corporate staff 16
cosmopolitan 76, 94, 95, 155
courage 62, 90
critical attitude 161
cross-cultural 16, 188
  transition 193
cross-cultural elaborations 154
cross-cultural person 154
cross-cultural research 193
cross-cultural training 130
cultural
  blending 57
  values of home 77
cultural awareness 193
cultural matching 198
cultural nuances 81
cultural references 96
cultural studies 203
culture 131

culture shock 16, 190
  at home 192
curiosity 77
customs 162

D

daughter 91
dead 195
death 158
defensive 43
denial 78
Derrida, Jacques 41
destiny 106
deviant 51
diagnosis 76, 191
diagnostic category 122
dialogue 60, 193
diary 35
difference 72, 115
  and belonging 50
different
  wanting to be 98
diplomatic 16
disenfranchisement 205
dislocation 202, 204
disorientation 19, 114, 133, 176
displacement 134, 153, 201
dispossessed 67
dissent 56
distress 209
disturbance 148
diversity 16, 77, 206
divorce 83
domestication 180
domocentrism 143
domophobia 143
dread 22
dreams 38, 94, 110
drifters 165

dual belonging 57
dwelling 156, 169, 172, 178

E

early relationships 83
earth 159, 179
economic crises 123
economic migrants 116
ecotourist 165
education 66
  and movement 107
eerie 37
Eliot, TS 19
émigré 199
empathy training 193
English 79
entitlement
  to home 150
environment 42
envy 116
equality 79
escape 57, 60, 78
  need to 59
ethnicity 78
everyday 157
everydayness 76
evocative description 121
excitement 37, 177
exclusion 36
exile 31, 167, 192, 199, 203
  self imposed in Budapest 35
exiles 200
existence 43, 59
existential 21, 109, 132
  facet of leaving 68
  need to return 95
existential anxiety 148
existential given 196

existential hero 170
existential inheritance 93
existentialists 156
existential migrant 7
   and Heideggerian analysis 170
   identity and leaving 46
existential migration 10, 26, 76, 122, 146, 174, 208
existential philosophy 156
existential shock 160
existential stagnation 113
existential therapy 198
existential tourism 165
exodus 52
ex-pat 102
ex-pat community 16, 64
expatriate 167, 203
expatriate managers 188
expectations 48
explanation 91
explanations 91

F

familiarity 93
family 82, 91
   chosen or constructed 89
   traditional 87
family dynamics 49, 88
family-oriented 64
far-sickness 52, 174
father 84, 85
feelings
   of the interview 32
felt sense 93
'fish out of water' 56
fluent 78
flux 153
forced evacuation 144

forced migration 147
foreign 21, 72
   within ourselves 186
foreigner
   despised 37
foreigners 38
foreign language 106
foreignness 185
foreign place 154
foreign postings 112
foreign students 173
fragmented life 58
freedom 55, 61
   from and to 184
   more important than belonging 64
Freud, Sigmund 21, 186, 195
The Uncanny 22
friends 75
friendships 98
Frodo 180
frustration 77
furusato 166
future 31

G

gay 51, 52
gender 51
Genesis 180
geographical process 109
ghost 37
global 15
global capitalism 123
global citizens 155
globalization 15, 130, 131, 152, 176, 211
global nomad 78, 116
global soul 168, 170
Global Soul 167

Goldenberg, Harriett 14
goodbye 39
gradual process
   of leaving 107
grandmother 90
Gray, Glen 156
Grinberg and Grinberg 23, 195
group migrations 147

H

healthy 192
Heidegger, Martin 21, 41, 130, 152, 156, 159, 169, 176, 196
   Building, Dwelling, Thinking 172
hero 44
heroic 44
hero's journey 177, 180
hero's return 44
historical context 96
history 180
Hofer, Johannes 173
Hoffman, Eva 13, 18, 200, 204
home 29, 97, 132, 147, 154, 164, 183, 205
   and refugees 197
   and therapy 198
   as geographical and psychological reality 102
   as interaction 103
   as rejecting 186
   exile and tranquillized 175
   is where I'm not 98
   leaving 29
   philosophy of 160

INDEX 223

return 92
visiting 80
home-body 160
homecoming 89, 115, 152
  and personal development 102
  in mythic literature 180
Homecoming 172, 176, 177, 178
  philosophy of 156
homecomrade 162
homeland 200
homelessness 38, 92, 101, 149, 168, 211
  and spirituality 68
homesick 99, 153
homesick immigrants 146
homesickness 52, 118, 169, 173, 174
hometown 94
homeworld 45, 101, 159, 160, 161, 162, 198
homing 154
homogeneity 75
homogeneous 45, 77
home culture 72
homogenization 211
horror 22
house 99, 142
  as museum 99
  as prison 100
human condition
  in myths 180
Huntington, June 20

I

identity 42, 45, 72, 76, 101, 131
  experimenting with 59
  marginality as a part

of 55
mixed, exotic 46
of parents 53
idiosyncrasy 77
immigrant
  parents 53
immigrants 16
immortals 177
imploded 43
inadequacy 116
inauthentic 53
incompetence 78
independence 21, 44, 51, 61, 83
individual psychology 194
inevitability
  of leaving 105
inferior 78
inferiority 38
inheritance 163
inherited 123
innate
  need to leave 54
insecure
  in childhood home 52
insecurity 16, 100
integrity 55
interaction 154
  between person and place 48
intercultural training 192, 193
internationalism 164, 212
internationalists 77, 115
international mobility 211
international resettlement 189
international students 24, 198
intersubjective 164
interview 60
intimate friendships 89
intuitive 69

involuntary migrant 103
isolation 35, 36, 43
Iyer, Pico 167

J

Japanese tourism 165
Jaspers, Karl 157
journey 177
judgement 94

K

knowledge-based 193
Kristeva, Julia 185
Kruks, Sonia 158

L

Lacan, Jacques 41
language 32, 77, 78, 81
Lawrence, DH 146
leaving 39, 194
leaving home
  likelihood of 91
Levinas, Emmanuel 41
liberation 73
lifeworld 159
liminal spaces 10
limit situation 158
literature 130, 180, 199
locals 38
locations
  residing in more than one 57
loneliness 31, 35
loneliness of travel 112
lonesomeness 180

longing 179
  for home 173
loss 31, 52, 168, 201, 209
Lost in Translation 13, 18
lostness 176, 182
loyalties 75

M

magic 59
maladaptation 87
management 192
Marcus, Clare Cooper 143
marginality 38, 53, 75
marginalization 50
marginalized 67, 76
market 176
mass
  the 'mass' at home 175
mature 111
meaning of home 210
mechanistic models 191
melancholia 90, 108
mental health 14, 192
mental space 63
Merleau-Ponty, Maurice 159
metaphors 24
middle-class 77
migrant workers 92, 198
migration 131
  begins before leaving 35
  of self-understanding 29
migration studies 27
migratory 163
mimic 53
minority 21
misappropriating 196
modernity 167
monolith 76
mortality 23

mortals 177
mother 100
  relations with 90
mothering 95
motivations 136, 194, 208
movement 153
multicultural 97
mundane 68, 72, 165
mundane life 66
mystery 29, 176
mystical 95, 143, 178
mythic 180
mythology 180
myths 130

N

national borders 155
nationalism 177
nature
  as home 156
need
  to escape 48
needs
  incompatible 48
nervous
  about leaving 106
neurotic 186
NGO 16
nightmare scenario 88
nomad 160, 167
nomadic 68
nonattachment 77
non-voluntary migration 56
normality 170
nostalgia 149, 167, 173
nostalgic 102, 164
nostalgic disorientation 148
not-at-home 175

not-belonging 49, 54, 162

O

ocnophilic 23, 194
O'Donohue, John 178
Odyssey 180
ontological insecurity 148
openness 51
  to life 75
oppressed 67
optimism 37
ordinary 59
ordinary and everyday 59
origin 78, 160, 176
Oslo 34
ostracized 55
otherness 68
Out of Place 13
outsider 45
outsiders
  and social networks 97

P

package holiday 165
pain
  of life 97
  of returning home 52
Pain, Stephanie 173
Papadopoulos, Renos 147, 197
paradox 114
parent
  relations with 85
parents
  and travel 59
parents 63
parents' attitude

to home 101
parochialism 168
partner 90
pathological 192
pathology 23, 191
peer acceptance 96
permanent transients 199
personality 87, 122
personal space 98
perspective 136
pessimistic 187
phenomenological unpacking 193
philobatic 23, 194
philosophical 49
philosophy 156, 185
physical place 93
pilgrim 166, 179
place 145
poetry 130
polarity 36
postmodern 15, 201
  view of self 133
potential 169
  of a unique self 43
power 79
preconceptions 73
pre-departure 193
predicament 115
predisposition 122
pretending
  and conformity 55
price
  of leaving 108
primary bonds 83
primordial homelessness 170
private inner world 58
private world 53
process
  view of migration 191
professionals 211
promised land 160

pronunciation 80
psychic 154
psychoanalysis 21, 186, 196
psychoanalyst 194
Psychoanalytic Perspectives on Migration and Exile 23
psychological 109
psychological problems 134
psychological traits 190
psychology 130
psychology of globalization 27
psychotherapy and counseling 16, 27, 130, 197
puritanical 73

Q

quotidian 77

R

race 57
  and belonging 57
racist 76
Rapport, Nigel 133, 152
reactive autonomy 185
Read, Peter 18, 144, 164, 191
realist
  view of self 133
reality 158
recognition 39
re-entry shock 190
reflective 65

reflective autonomy 184
reflective space 60
refugee 147, 167, 197
refugees 16, 92, 123, 192, 198
regret 31
reintegration 190
reinvent
  oneself 55
rejection 43
  of home culture 55
relationship 38, 58, 81
relax
  at home 93
religious fundamentalism 177
relocation 26
relocation consulting 78
research 60
resentment 115
resettling 89
return 31, 92, 95, 189
returnee 175
returning 110, 115
  as retiring from life 100
returning home 65, 92
Returning to Nothing 18
risk factors 191
rite of passage 102, 104
Ritivoi, Andreea 132
rituals 162
Rivett, Carole 19
rootedness 145
root envy 200
rootless 47
rootlessness 19, 136, 146
roots 97, 199

S

sacrament of homecoming 104
sacred time 97
Said, Edward 13, 203, 204
scepticism 25
secondary motivations 61
secret 196
security 16, 75
sedentary 44, 163
sedentary adventure 60
self 42, 135
   and language 80
   and other 42
   compromised 53
   fragile sense of 47
self-acceptance 96
self-discovery 177
self-indulgent 177
self-in-migration 132
self-reliance 115
self-worth 44
sensitivities 49, 184
sensitizing 34
settlement 204
settling 117
sexuality 52
shame 35, 51, 113, 116
siblings 48, 58, 85
silence 35
Simic, Charles 205
similarity 72, 73
   within difference 76
sleep deprivation 190
social justice 53, 67, 76
social network 108
social norms 57
sociologists 191
soldiers 173
solitary 32, 147, 155
solitary respite 58
solitude 38, 97
sorrow 37
sorrow of estrangement 205
soul 144
soul-destroying 77
space 59, 61, 63
   and relationship 42
   search for 42
special
   feeling of being 72
special status 175
spiritual 89, 166, 178
   practice 68
spiritual dimension 68
spirituality 130
spouse 123
stage theories 190
statelessness 38
Steinbock, Anthony 159, 162, 163
stereotype 47
stifling
   hometown 55
strange 196
stranger 50, 108
stranger in a familiar land 105
strangers 94
stress 190
study 60
suburbia 146
suffocated 59
   at home 56
suffocating
   belonging 48
suffocation 65
superficial 78
superiority
   towards those who stay 116
symbol 80

T

taboo 85
taken-for-granted 42
television 176
terrain 160
The Lord of the Rings 180
theory 83
therapeutic 19, 197
therapeutic sessions 32
therapeutic tourism 165, 170
therapist 42
therapy 197
The Uncanny 195
time
   return as going back in time 102
time travel 104, 200
tolerant
   personality 189
Tolkien, JRR 180
tourism 164
tourism studies 130
tourist 164
tradition 159
traditional cultures 45
tragic 180
trailing families 16
trailing partner 123
tranquilizing 66
tranquillized 25
transcendent 68
transformation 177
transformative 177
transience 89
transit camps 197
transition 33
transpersonal 68
trauma 197
travel 44, 58, 59, 76
travelling 65
tribalism 177

tribe 10, 62, 81, 162, 180
truths
   ultimate and contextual 97
twenty-first century 165, 176

U

uncanniness 169
uncanny 21, 94, 95, 103, 114, 157, 186
uncertainties 169
unconscious 196
understood
   importance of being understood 115
unfamiliar 72
unheimlich 21, 22, 114, 154, 160, 163, 164, 169, 186, 195
uniqueness 47
university
   as excuse to leave 107
unlived life 103, 104
unrooted 199

V

values 163
van Manen, Max 41
vicious circle
   of belonging and suffocation 58
voice
   following one's own 62
voluntary 19
voluntary migrant 27
voluntary migrants 14

voluntary migration 195, 209

W

wanderer 179
wanderlusts 165
war 99
W-curve 190
Weber, Zita 19
welcome 51
Winning, Anne 174
world economy 202

X

xenophobia 186

Y

yearning 169

Made in the USA
Las Vegas, NV
13 May 2024